AN ALLEGORY FOR MICHAEL

Serpent, Lion, Dragon, Phoenix

Anthony Michael

Gungnir Press

Copyright © 2023 Anthony Michael D'Abarno

All rights reserved

No part of this book may be reproduced, or stored in a retrieval system, or transmitted in any form or by any means, electronic, mechanical, photocopying, recording, or otherwise, without express written permission of the publisher.

ISBN:9798872845744

Cover design by: Snir Alayof
Printed in the United States of America

To Michael,
As a son receiving the Word from his father, use this moral compass to navigate beyond good and evil. We share the same name—Michael—in honor of God's greatest champion. Aim your flaming arrows at the devil's heart, and together, we shall rejoice in the Holy Trinity.
Amen

PROLOGUE

Serpents Among the Rubble

I dedicate this work to my son, Michael, family, friends, the world, and God. As a father communicating the Word to his son, join me in preserving generational wisdom while aiming toward the Holy Trinity. Hopefully, these words will lay the foundation for our collective future, providing a moral compass with an impeccable aim for our sons and daughters. God knows they need one now more than ever, so He asked me to deliver you this flaming arrow. It is an arrow that cannot miss its target, much like the Spear of Destiny or the flaming sword that guards the Tree of Life. That arrow is this converted atheist's prayer. That arrow is a rhetorical question that honors Archangel Michael and God:

Who is like God?

In the shadows of modern times, where the echoes of spiritual tyranny resonate akin to the oppressive reign of the pharaohs, I find myself compelled to inscribe the pages of this tome. Much like Moses, who faced the tyrannical grip of an empire that sought to dominate not only the physical realm but also the spirit of its people, I am stirred by a profound calling to navigate the tumultuous desert of our contemporary existence.

The genesis of this work emerged not from stone tablets atop Mount Sinai but from the paper peaks of ancient wisdom. That wisdom contrasted against the digital peaks of the internet, where the clamor of voices and the cacophony of ideas can either illuminate the path to enlightenment or plunge one into the abyss of confusion. As if guided by an unseen hand, I received a vision—an ethereal beckoning to ascend a metaphorical mountain, where, at its summit, I would encounter not tablets of stone but a mirror reflecting the virtues essential for leading humanity out of the bewildering wilderness of the internet.

In the solitude of that sacred ascent, I communed with God to receive a transcendental principle that binds these virtues into a harmonious symphony of guidance. Like Moses, who received divine revelations on the mountain, I discovered a profound connection between these virtues. This connection transcends the mundane and taps into the very essence of our shared humanity.

As I inscribe these revelations, I am acutely aware of the responsibility bestowed upon me—akin to that of a father imparting wisdom to his son. With a heart overflowing with love and an unwavering commitment to humanity and God, I dedicate this work to my son, Michael, as a testament to the enduring legacy of wisdom passed from one generation to the next.

To my family, whose unwavering support has been the cornerstone of my journey, and to my friends, who have stood as pillars of strength through the trials of creation, this work is a tribute to the power of communal bonds. To the whole world, in the spirit of Moses, I extend an invitation to partake in the journey outlined within these pages—a journey toward enlightenment, understanding, and collective liberation from the deserts of misinformation that shroud the digital landscape.

Above all, this dedication extends to God—the silent orchestrator of our destinies and the source of inspiration that guided my pen. In this endeavor, I am but a vessel, humbly embracing the charge to illuminate the path toward a promised land where virtue reigns supreme over the dark digital landscape and the echoes of wisdom resound through the annals of time. Let this work be a beacon of light in the encroaching shadows, an offering to all who seek clarity amid the chaos of the virtual expanse.

When Friedrich Nietzsche—the 19th-century German philosopher who falsely proclaimed "God is dead"—destroyed morality with a philosophical hammer, all he left behind was the rubble of a fallen temple. Now, serpents slither through the rubble, seeking to tempt lost souls with a poison apple. Therefore, let us analyze the fallout before rebuilding, calling out the serpents for their viciousness. We aim to obliterate Nietzsche's immoral philosophy and all the serpents that slither around like scavengers through the rubble.

I don't claim to be a prophet. I don't even claim to know the whole truth, but I do know some parts. Don't we all? It's an important distinction because it implies that truth can still be derived by following fragments of wisdom like clues, merging them with empirical evidence. Join me as we travel down a rabbit hole of knowledge and wisdom. Dig down below what you know into what you don't. When you no longer know, the only remaining insight is that you don't know, so the only wise thing to do is learn, aiming at the whole through a combination of logical deduction and induction. By aiming at dual halves of the truth, our arrows land nearer to the center of the whole, for all paths converge, whether *a priori* or *a posteriori*.

How do individuals define their purpose without relying on religious frameworks in a society that often emphasizes secular values? The snakes among the rubble of our fallen temple make you believe you can create your own values out of thin air. They do so based on perverted morality—a satanic mode of valuation—enslaving their followers through deception, wearing masks that suit the impulsive ethos of the era to enrich themselves, driven by Nietzsche's will to power. Led astray through either blind faith or complete ignorance, their acolytes don't even know they've been enslaved. They happily wear their chains as they chase the allure of transhumanism, running after a hedonistic carrot like a herd of livestock. That is what atheism necessarily offers us in the absence of religion.

Without a religious moral compass, how does society establish and justify ethical standards, and how do these standards adapt to changing norms? The snakes among the rubble make you believe individuals should follow their own moral compass. Their atheist logic tells us the north is the south and the south is the north, always resulting in the opposite conclusion. They tell us that we don't need God, claiming "God is dead," yet when we follow their directions, we end up lost in satanism instead. What happens then? They change the definition of words, so they might retreat back to religion without contradicting themselves. That is how the atheist moral compass establishes and justifies ethical standards by misappropriating semantics to change their aim when it suits them.

As technology continues to shape human experiences, how does an atheist worldview grapple with questions of identity, consciousness, and the potential for existential threats posed by technology? The snakes among the rubble make you believe in contradiction—*deus ex machina*. They tell us to embrace individuality, manipulating us through impulse and emotion using evermore powerful technology, wielding cognitive dissonance as a weapon while leading us like lambs to the slaughter. Once our souls have been dyed by their insatiable bloodlust, they push us to the edge of a cliff and implore us to do the exact opposite of embracing individuality—sacrifice our identity for a collective owned and operated by transhumanist pharaohs. Those transhumanists keep their slaves in line, constantly threatening the eradication of humanity, with the ultimate threat: mutually assured destruction through thermonuclear war. That is how atheism grapples with the identity of humankind by sacrificing it on the altar of a technocentric tyranny that aims, above all else, to find God in the machine.

Like a vampire, that machine powers itself on human blood. Like a demon, that machine powers itself on human souls. Yet they find no God in that machine, only His wrath encapsulated by a nuclear bomb.

In a society where political affiliations often replace religious identity, how can atheists contribute to fostering unity and dialogue in the face of ideological differences? The snakes among the rubble make you believe political harmony can be achieved without a unifying moral principle beyond ourselves. They tell us we should rally behind political causes based on personal identity, failing to recognize that tribes organize around dogma, too. While arguing that religious dogma necessarily leads to the abuse of power, they downplay the adverse effects of tribal dogma, ignoring the evidence that tribalization is far more abusive. Thus, they endlessly sacrifice their enemies as effigies to the cult of personality, burning their political opponents at the stake to glorify their own image, reducing God to class, gender, and ethnicity.

I have no doubt they'll do the same to me, should my perspective find purchase within the collective psyche. The witches will call me a witch and burn me at the stake. That is how atheists contribute to unification in our current political landscape by promoting a division of tribes based on their physical properties—segregation—while offering those segregated tribes unity only in the destruction of their political rivals.

I made peace with that sacrifice long ago, for the technocratic pharaohs who walk upon the backs of the common people have left us no other choice. Someone must challenge their ignorant, abusive, atheist, immoral, and evil will to power. Someone must lead the world out of the vast desert of the internet, where their serpents deceive us with the knowledge of good and evil, preying upon our greatest fears, including thermonuclear war. Witches and wizards poison us with snake oil, vampires suck our blood, and demons harvest our spirits, possessing our hearts and minds from within, dyeing our souls until we become serpents, the embodiment of Satan.

When will the madness end?

True power resides in conquering fears—this and more

shall be revealed in the following pages—and the ultimate manifestation of power is found in transcendental self-sacrifice. Nietzsche's concept of the will to power aligns with what can be described as *virtue signaling*—a deceptive projection of false truths aimed at gaining power—and *gaslighting*. Virtue signaling combines pity and pride with the subjugation of virtue through lies while gaslighting insidiously manipulates by perpetuating false narratives and making one question reality. They are the devil's tools. Those who engage in virtue signaling and gaslighting distort truths, turning reality on its head and confounding us through inversion and division. They argue that we're the ones who killed God when, in fact, they're the ones who perpetrated the crime.

Knowledge of good and evil is not a teachable concept, unlike what the serpents make you believe, but an immanent and divine gift from God. Embodied as a *syzygy* —the reunification of Adam and Eve in Jesus's sacrifice—we discover the Holy Trinity. That syzygy can be defined in an astronomical, psychological, and biblical sense—transcendental communication between the conscious and unconscious mind, resulting in the alignment of three heavenly bodies as one— which we will do in more detail before the conclusion of our journey.

Syzygy is inverted and divided by the serpent's tricks, becoming a schism of infinite dualities through a selfish and acquisitive mind. Morality, when observed through the lens of desire or elevated as a false idol, leads to the death of God, fragmenting the whole into paradoxical halves. Then those halves infinitely divide into polarized atoms and binary subatomic quanta, which desperately seek reunification. Endless fission leads to inevitable nuclear fusion and the revelation of God's true power. Eventually, we'll blow ourselves up; it's the only logical conclusion in the absence of God. Is it merely a coincidence that Nietzsche's atheism, a precursor to postmodernism, led us to the thermonuclear bomb?

However, pursuing virtue without a satanic passion

for the acquisition of false idols results in the resurrection, accepting all dualistic parts as an integrated whole. Thus, virtue signaling attempts to rewrite the commandments of the universe and God, straying from the natural order of syzygy.

While virtue signaling destroys morality through inversion, gaslighting misappropriates our deepest existential fears and uses them against us to divide us. Fear reflects evil by destroying an image of what is most cherished, and the serpent exploits this image to manipulate and distort reality. Again, the threat of mutually assured destruction, symbolized by the thermonuclear bomb, represents the sum of all fears, destroying all of humanity. Sacrificing cherished images becomes the ultimate antidote to this manipulation. The devil seeks to dismantle God's creation, employing division through individualism as his greatest weapon. Acknowledging the devil's game, adopting its mask, and delving into its mindset constitute nonviolent spiritual warfare—the remedy to prevent mutually assured destruction. *Logos*—reasoned discourse and the divine Word—becomes necessary to navigate this spiritual battleground of good and evil by emphasizing differences rather than similarities with Satan.

It's not how you are alike that shapes reality. It's how you are different, and that difference is embodied in syzygy.

To achieve the greatest good and embody the image of God, one must sacrifice the best part of oneself to the worst, thereby preventing the fall into infinite paradoxical dualities of false idols. This warning against obsession over dualities (Heaven and Hell, pleasure and pain, good and evil, etc.) is crucial. Self-conscious sacrifice transcends conventional notions of duality, encouraging a focus on the metagame. This strategy rises above opposites and forms a new shared consciousness with God. While evil pursues the will to power by inverting good and evil, God's love is channeled through the choice to sacrifice, shielding one from the satanic corruption of power. God invites us to find power but advocates for its non-exploitative use. In the grand metagame of existence, the call is to play and win, overcoming the will to abuse power.

In the postmodern age, thermonuclear war always looms on the horizon. Yet, this revelation from God offers hope that, through a syzygy of conscious-unconscious arguments, the destructive aspect of atheism will be annihilated by its own logic. Since I've been tasked to deliver this message, I have faith that we can preserve our free will without destroying ourselves through God. So please don't shoot the messenger, and heed my arguments with an open mind as I present God's final admonition to the world.

Specific individuals—you already know who they are, so I don't need to tell you their names—who share this sentiment have penetrated the collective psyche with their reasoned discourse, acting as lightning rods of the Logos. They play the metagame for "Team Humanity," presently waging a spiritual war against transhumanist technocrats. Though I hope they will join us in our mission, I would rather not use their names and drag them into this sacrifice against their will. Still, their wisdom offers the only beacon of hope amid the darkness of the desert, guiding us toward truth as an antidote for fear. Together, let us continue their courageous work, advancing deep into enemy territory to overthrow our abusers through nonviolent resistance and common purpose, our aim guided by faith in God. Thus, we will thoroughly deconstruct Nietzsche's will to power through a syzygy of conscious and unconscious arguments, smiting his atheist philosophy with a lightning bolt of Logos and immolating the serpents who slither among the rubble with our flaming arrows.

CHAPTER ONE

The Allegory

"Well, I stand up next to a mountain, and I chop it down with the edge of my hand."

—JIMI HENDRIX, "VOODOO CHILD (SLIGHT RETURN)"

Can you trust your senses and emotions? Do you trust your brain with one hundred percent accuracy? Do you believe you're a rational thinker? I assume you do, or else that would mean you think you're irrational, which is a different problem. What is rationality, anyway? What do you aim for, pleasure and avoidance of pain? If not, what else, truth, power, or perhaps even transcendence? Or are you completely and utterly lost among the meaningless, random, and hopeless chaos of a universe born from nothing?

Answer these questions honestly, and you'll soon discover that you know far less than you first assumed. How you answer these questions shapes more than just your view of reality; it colors your morality, dyeing the fabric of your soul. Do you even have a soul, or are you just a meat machine that eternally decomposes when you die? Are you accidentally assembled from nothing and inevitably dissolved into nothing, recycled by a perpetual thermodynamic equilibrium without origin, a victim of a cosmic crematorium? If you can't even begin to answer them, it's a sign you must continue reading.

Your very soul may depend upon it.

We are about to climb a mountain—a philosophical Mount Everest. Then, in the spirit of Jimi Hendrix, we'll attempt to "chop it down." As your spirit guide, I've already ascended a metaphysical Mount Sinai for you to acquire the wisdom that will help us rebuild when the rubble settles. Aim toward strength beyond yourself, and you will not quit when the journey gets hard.

Let us first establish a base camp, a place to retreat when fear and confusion cloud our minds like a blizzard, a foundation for wisdom and clarity as we embark upon this journey together. Should you lose sight of your target, return to base camp until you are ready to begin anew, and I'll be waiting for you.

If, however, your will shatters, the act of quitting shall haunt you like a specter for eternity. I invoke this curse out of duty and necessity rather than viciousness, for those few who reach the pinnacle of the mountain will know that voodoo has no power over an indomitable spirit. Our world is filled with curses, venomous words dripping from serpents' fangs, contagious as an infection, seeping into our souls to become tainted thoughts that wrap their twisted tentacles around our brains, moving our unconscious bodies against ourselves by impulse. Thus, we become slaves, bound by chains of negativity and superstition.

The antidote awaits at the top of the mountain. Will you join me in acquiring it? Do you have what it takes?

Our base camp is not a physical place. Instead, it is a metaphysical one fashioned from words and archetypes, an allegory rooted in psychology, philosophy, and religion. Let the allegory communicate with your unconscious mind. Only then will the logical arguments that follow resonate between the conscious and unconscious halves of yourself.

The allegory begins with a man walking through a desert,

carrying a bag of gold to a dragon that awaits at the top of a mountain. He is you. He is me. He is all of us. Let us, therefore, follow him along his journey.

A man looks toward the mountain on the horizon, wiping the sweat from his brow, the blazing sun baking the sand beneath his bare feet. Yet he marches onward, carrying a bag overflowing with gold slung across his back. He cannot stop, for the lives of all those back home—everyone and everything he knows and loves—depend on it.

The gold represents the collective wealth of his village, an annual tithe demanded by a dragon who dwells atop the mountain. The dragon descends each year, threatening the villagers with death by fire and demanding payment for his lordship. Thus, he hoards their gold all for himself, adorning himself with glittering scales inscribed with the countless laws of his people.

Some worship the dragon as a protector and willingly offer him their gold. Others fear him as a god, while their opponents think him an imposter. Regardless of their beliefs, they always follow his laws. They always pay the tithe.

Now, the bag of gold grows evermore burdensome with each step, and the man trudges through the desert alone, never losing sight of the mountain on the horizon, which moves ever further beyond his reach. Is it a mirage? The sun rises and sets many times during his journey until he loses track of time. Hunger, thirst, and pain hammer away at his spirit with each footfall. His spine bends, nearly breaking, under the weight of his burden until the rain comes.

A storm cloud forms overhead, and lightning streaks the sky. Then the man lays down his burden, at last, and dances as the rain falls upon him. He opens his mouth toward the heavens and drinks, praising God for such good fortune. He loses himself in joy, and that's when thunder strikes.

A bolt of light arcs down from Heaven and smites the man—*BOOM!* His vision goes white before turning dark, and a thunderous roar rings in his ears, unlike anything he has ever heard. For a moment, he lies there unconscious. When he awakes, he hears a voice issue this warning:

"You mustn't venture to climb the mountain nor eat fruit from the tree at its peak, and you mustn't touch it, or you will die."

The man opens his eyes, surprised to find himself transformed. He rises from the sand not as a man but as a camel. Still, he carries the bag of gold upon his humped back. Furthermore, he now stands at the mountain's base, no longer miles away.

He glances up at the top of the mountain beyond the clouds, letting the rain wash over him, and recalls the warning:

You mustn't venture to climb the mountain nor eat fruit from the tree at its peak, and you mustn't touch it, or you will die.

What fruit, he wonders. *What tree? Who is it that speaks to me? Am I dreaming? Am I dead? Or was it someone else, perhaps even God?*

"Pst," another voice says, different from the first. "Pst, down here."

Once a man, the camel looks down to find a fox that emerges from the shadows. The fox rolls an apple in the sand, offering it to the camel.

"You bring tithes to the dragon who lives atop the mountain," says the fox, "but what if I told you there was another way to save yourself and your city? What would you be willing to do to keep everyone and everything you know and love safe, now and always? What if I told you there was a way to slay the dragon?"

"I'd first ask who you are," says the camel, "then what do you want, and then how... how did I get here? And how do I slay the dragon?"

"Eat the apple," says the fox, rolling it toward the camel with its snout. "When you eat the apple, all these mysteries and more will reveal themselves before your eyes."

"But what about the voice," says the camel after deep contemplation, trying in vain to resist the temptation, "the one that awoke me from slumber. It said not to climb the mountain nor eat the fruit from the tree at its peak, or else I would die. Where did you get that apple anyway, out here in the desert?"

The fox laughs, saying, "Poor creature, can't you see you've been deceived? The dragon smote you with lightning as soon as he saw you approach his heavenly home, transforming you into a camel with his magic. You heard his voice issue a warning from on high. He hopes you will never know the secret of his power. That's why I stole the apple from his tree so that I might give it to someone worthy like you."

"The secret?"

"Yes," says the fox, "the secret. Of all the treasures the dragon hoards, he guards this secret above all others. But this secret can only be revealed once you know the dragon's power, which can only be obtained by eating the fruit from the tree under which the dragon slumbers."

The words resonate with the camel's conscience as he recalls his human wife's face. He remembers how she cried when he left home to deliver the dragon's tithe and the fear in her voice. At that moment, he decides to slay the dragon once and for all. So he picks up the apple and takes a bite.

The fox laughs again, and the laughter melts into a hiss.

Before the camel's eyes, a veil reveals the secret beyond. Reality itself turns on its head, and the mountain sinks to become the darkest volcanic abyss, an unfathomable fissure in the earth. The fox is not a fox, no more than he is a camel. Instead, he realizes that he was a lion wearing a camel's mask all along, and the fox was nothing more than a serpent wearing a fox's mask.

"What have you done to me," says the lion, throwing off his camel's mask, mane blowing in the wind. "Was this all just a lie, you snake!"

"No," says the serpent with a hiss, "not at all. It wasn't me, remember, but the dragon who did this to you. He's the one who lies. After all, you're not dead yet."

"I suppose you're right," says the lion, gazing down into the abyss, heart full of dread, "but if that's so, tell me now how to slay the dragon."

"Very well," says the serpent, "follow me. To ascend, you must first descend. As above, so below."

The lion follows the serpent into the abyss. Like the mirage in the desert, the descent seems endless. Yet, eventually, the lion and the serpent reach the bottom, where the dragon sleeps coiled around the base of an apple tree. The only light down here shines from the dragon's countless gilded scales, fashioned from gold coins inscribed with laws, flickering like torchlight and casting shadows across the tree's boughs. A standing mirror framed in gold faces the dragon for his gazing pleasure.

"You see that magic mirror," says the serpent, whispering in the lion's ear. "That's how the dragon sees and observes all of existence, past, present, and future, but first, he must eat the tree's fruit to wield such power. You, too, may look in the mirror to discover the secret now that you've acquired the taste."

Following the serpent, the lion approaches the mirror, prowling not to wake the dragon. As the dragon shifts in sleep or draws breath, the clinking and clamoring of its scales echo throughout the darkness, ominous warnings to be sure. Undaunted, the courageous lion arrives before the mirror to be greeted by his reflection.

What he sees almost sends him running, for yet another veil vanishes from his eyes.

Between the serpent and the dragon, the lion's reflection gazes up in terror at the human version of himself hanging from the tree. The bones of the man's predecessors litter the ground below, their owners devoured by the dragon. How long has he been up there? Nine hours, or even nine days? The thirst, hunger, and pain he endured while walking through the desert pales in comparison to this torture. He wants to scream, though he resists for fear of waking the dragon.

Despite his best efforts, it's the serpent who ultimately betrays him.

"My lord," says the serpent, hissing in the dragon's ear, "please, forgive me… but I've brought you your servant at last. As you can see, he failed the test."

One giant eye shoots open behind the lion, reflected in the mirror. The pupil narrows, focusing on the lion standing there, and then the dragon rises. The sound of so many scales jangling sends a shiver down the lion's spine. A song of the damned commands him to obey as a legion of screaming faces swarms out of the abyss, reciting the dragon's laws.

Entranced, the lion can't turn away from the mirror, but still, he manages to say to the serpent, "Traitor! How could you? You've been working together all along, haven't you?"

"Of course," says the dragon, rising from slumber, a cacophony of chiming scales, "for in the end, we're all one, and your end is nigh. What makes you think you can slay me, your god?"

Though the dragon's voice booms with authority, the lion at once knows it differs from the voice he heard after being struck by lightning. Thus, the man dangling from the tree cries out, "Don't listen to him! They're nothing but false idols, these petty little lords of inversion and division. Look in the mirror. He's hidden the only arrow behind the glass capable of piercing his gilded heart."

"Silence!"

The dragon turns to face the man dangling from the tree, whose arms and legs are bound and stretched by chains linked to the branches.

"When I found you at the base of the mountain, struck by lightning, you were on the brink of death," says the dragon, seething with rage until smoke billows from his nostrils, "so I brought you here. I saved you, and this is how you repay me? Still, I'm a glorious god… and should you pass my test, all shall be forgiven. There is no absolute truth, only power, which I alone can grant you. Now, I ask only that you kneel before me. Praise me as your god, and that power shall become yours."

Watching everything transpire, a mere spectator looking in the mirror, the lion witnesses two masks appear at his feet. One is the camel mask he wore before, and the other is the fox mask the serpent wore. Furthermore, he watches the four of them align, their reflections superimposed to become one—serpent, lion, dragon, and hanging man—and a vision materializes before his eyes. What strange magic...

The lion makes his choice, dawning the fox mask, and to his surprise, a bow and flaming arrow appear in its place. Now, he sees that they are all one by their superimposed reflections. At that moment, he knows what he must do. He, too, must die to slay the dragon. Thus, he takes up the bow, notches the arrow, and aims it at the heart of the hanging man.

When he sees this, the hanging man screams, "My God, my God, why hast thou forsaken me?"

The lion releases the arrow, striking himself in the heart. Enraged, the dragon belches flame when neither man nor lion kneels, engulfing the tree in fire, and the man burns alive, his screams echoing through the abyss, mirrored in the gilded faces that scream the dragon's laws. The flames grow, burning brighter and hotter, and a lake of fire encircles the ground upon which they stand. Soon, the burning tree turns to ash, crumbling into a pile of soot, yet an egg remains concealed beneath in its place.

"Look what you've done, you fool. You missed the mark, and now you'll suffer the consequences," says the dragon, spinning to confront the lion, who notices that his gilded scales can no longer take the heat. The screaming faces drip like candle wax as the conflagration swells around them. "Oh, I'll make you pay for such blasphemy. How dare you attempt to slay me, your god!"

"You can't hurt me anymore," says the lion, voice booming across the lake of fire," and, no, I didn't miss... for as you said, we're all one. Thus, if you harm me, you hurt yourself.

Father, forgive us, for we know not what we do."

With those words, the egg cracks open, and a phoenix emerges from the pile of soot. The dragon roars, taking flight, and the lion sees fear fill the dragon's eyes. Yet his wings, now mostly melted, can no longer support his weight, and despite how hard he tries, he can't escape the lake of fire. Instead, he turns toward the phoenix and unleashes one last gasp of fire and fury.

Through the flames, the phoenix soars toward the dragon's heart. Like an arrow, his beak pierces the bullseye, and the dragon falls, showering gold coins across the firmament of Heaven. What happens next is indeed a sight to behold, for the phoenix continues its path skyward, a meteor of gold and fire illuminating the abyss and revealing the belly of a volcano. The lake of fire belches lava forth, and the volcano erupts.

Thus, the man's dream ends in an explosion of fire and brimstone. When he awakes, the desert transforms into a paradise.

The man blinks, hardly believing his eyes. He squints at the mountain on the horizon, now sundered by the volcanic eruption still billowing smoke into the atmosphere. Golden droplets of rain shower the flourishing gardens around him, which replace the sand. A great wall with golden gates separates him from the inner garden, blossoming with beauty beyond words.

Then he notices the bag of gold spilled across the ground as he scrambles to his feet. He shakes his head in disbelief, thinking this is just another dream. However, he soon realizes the gold coins have changed.

He falls to his knees, sifting the coins in search of meaning. Is this all that's left of the dragon, just his scales? He turns a coin over in his hands for closer inspection, and upon it, a new law is inscribed:

Only through sacrifice can one truly know... On one side of the coin, the inscription ends with *virtue*; on the other, it ends with *vice.* When he flips the coin, however, the two words merge to become one: *God*.

He continues sifting, checking that each coin has the same inscription, which they do. However, he discovers something else when he reaches deeper into the bag of gold. There, he finds the bow and arrow. More coins pour onto the ground as he removes them in his excitement. He leaps to his feet, exhilarated by the discovery. The thought of so much power at his fingertips nearly consumes him. However, he remembers his journey's trials and tribulations thus far. He finds new meaning in those memories.

Only through sacrifice...

Therefore, he notches the arrow, which bursts into flame, draws back the bowstring, aiming toward Heaven, and speaks directly to God, "You knew I would climb the mountain, didn't you? You knew I would eat the apple, too? But if so, why? Why would You let me act against Your will, especially when You knew I would?"

"I made you in My image," says God. "I gave you free will. That necessarily implies the burden of choice falls upon you, child. And you alone must bear that burden on My behalf. I neither could nor should stop you, lest I contradict Myself. More importantly, I knew either way that you would slay the dragon. As a logical self-simulation, I already ran that simulation. The alternative didn't compute."

"Forgive me, Father," says the man, releasing the flaming arrow toward Heaven. "For I knew not what I did. Therefore, let this final sacrifice prove my repentance. Now I relinquish the dragon's power in Your name."

The fiery arrow arcs across Heaven like a shooting star, transforming midair and taking flight as a phoenix that disappears beyond the horizon, engulfed by the sun's glare. Hinges creak, and the man looks down, surprised to find the golden gateway into paradise has opened. Without another word, he collects the dragon's scales, upon which God's law is written, to bring his newfound wisdom back to his people. Thus, he walks into paradise with the bag of gold slung across his back and the golden gates close behind him.

Let the imagery in this allegory soak your unconscious mind in its meaning before moving forward. In subsequent chapters, we will explain why simultaneously engaging your mind's conscious and unconscious aspects is necessary to arrive at truth. Now, we are primed to begin our journey. If nothing else, you will acquire nearly 200 quotes along the way filled with life-changing wisdom from six of history's greatest philosophers.

We ascend this mountain together, consciously engaging in philosophy to acquire the antidote against our present cultural and spiritual decline. First, we will disprove the philosophy of Friedrich Nietzsche, particularly his concept of the "will to power." We will do so not by going against the grain of his logic but quite the contrary. We will follow his prescription of embracing the will to power by constructing our own *Übermensch* (Overman or Superman), using the words of philosophers who attempted to do something similar, six in total, half Eastern philosophers and the other half Western, mostly pre-Christian or non-Christian. These philosophers come from cultures or perspectives that adhere more closely to Nietzsche's knightly-aristocratic mode of valuation rather than the priestly mode of valuation. For if Nietzsche's logic is sound, we certainly cannot arrive back at the image of God, exemplified by Jesus Christ, when constructing the Übermensch, lest God will be resurrected and Nietzsche's logic shattered. After all, it was Nietzsche who falsely proclaimed, "God is dead. God remains dead. And we have killed him."

CHAPTER TWO

The Semantic Shell Game

As previously explained, the allegory is our base camp—the foundation of our unconscious argument. Now, let's dive into the conscious portion of our journey with a similar aim, arriving nearer the truth and returning to base camp when necessary.

First, we must establish the core tenets of Nietzsche's brand of philosophy. Of these, there are four: 1.) the will to power, 2.) the Übermensch, 3.) the idea of eternal return, and 4.) philosophical aestheticism—the conception of art and aesthetics playing a central and necessary role in philosophy. However, before we briefly define the first two in more detail, we must also address his writing style, laden with poetry, metaphors, and aphorisms, exemplifying the last core tenet of philosophical aestheticism. Altogether, this unique style frames his arguments in literary filagree, which is much more appropriate for communication with the unconscious rather than the conscious mind. In this regard, I believe he achieved his most profound success, which we will touch upon later in our discussion about truth emerging from and transcending duality as divine syzygy.

Unfortunately, Nietzsche was only half right, yet one cannot deny his appeal to the unconscious. For the sake of our argument, we'll not waste precious time and therefore assume his ideas of eternal return and philosophical aestheticism are correct, focusing instead on the will to power and the Übermensch.

Let us first define the will to power: "It is power, this new virtue; it is a ruling idea, and around it a subtle soul: a golden sun, and around it the serpent of knowledge."

Nietzsche claimed that nearly all morality derived from a priestly mode of valuation is fundamentally flawed because it emerged through the subversion and inversion of a knightly-aristocratic mode of valuation, leading to a slave revolt, self-deception, or, even worse, herd mentality, which undermines itself, is unhealthy, and stifles greatness. Distilled into simpler terms, he believed Christian morality was evil because it parasitized the greatness of the Roman Empire.

"You have served the people and the people's superstitions, all you famous philosophers!" he says in *Thus Spoke Zarathrustra*. "You have *not* served truth."

More specifically, he believed the "will to truth" expressed by his predecessors was a facade, nothing more than a glorified pursuit of power for their benefit.

"That is your entire will, you wisest men; it is a will to power; and that is so even when you talk of good and evil and of the assessment of values."

As he saw it, the origin of their will corrupted everything it touched beyond repair; it somehow corrupted despite empowering the priests and philosophers he accused of infecting the minds of the masses.

"You exert power with your values and doctrines of good and evil, you assessors of values; and this is your hidden love and the glittering, trembling, and overflowing of your souls.

"But a mightier power and a new overcoming grow from out your values: egg and egg-shell break against them.

"And he who has to be a creator in good and evil, truly, has first to be a destroyer and break values."

But how could that be considered good advice if the will to power serves as the origin for creating all morals and values in the first place, including those new ones he seeks as their replacements? Could his perspective be nothing more than projection and self-incrimination?

Nevertheless, he endeavored to shatter everything built upon the supposedly shaky foundation of the will to truth —Western civilization—with a philosophical hammer, only to invite all the free spirits of the world to rebuild their own set of morals and values anew.

"The good and just call me the destroyer of morals: my story is immoral."

Barely sharing any insight into how they should do so, he only offered them the Übermensch—a false idol to replace the God he thought they had killed—leaving his followers aimless and blind as they sifted through the rubble of Western civilization.

"You should create a higher body, a first motion, a self-propelling wheel—you should create a creator."

Is there anything more immoral than what he single-handedly did to our culture? Is there any desire more irrational?

Let's deconstruct the will to power further by unraveling its logically inconsistent threads before we move on to the Übermensch. It's debatable whether Nietzsche accomplished his goal of proving the will to truth is, in actuality, the will to power. By his estimation, the will to truth originated from the will to power, which doesn't change the possibility that one can have disharmonious intentions between the conscious and unconscious, leading to unintended consequences. Speaking metaphorically, an arrow and target are not the same, and the outcome is unknowable with certainty by only knowing the unconscious origin or aim, especially considering that consciousness plays a much more significant role in a rational man's life.

But let's assume he was successful. That would not negate the power contained in the wisdom of past philosophers—no, quite the contrary—even if it represents a fragment or mere reflection of the whole truth.

In fact, by playing a shell game with origin and intent,

cause-and-effect, and ontology and teleology, switching the words "truth" and "power" to distract us from the overall positive effects of Western morality regardless of their creators' original conscious or unconscious intent, he hijacked millennia of logic upon which to prop up his brand of philosophy and boost his own power without actually refuting much of their original logic. He barely even attempted, devoting a few paragraphs to each philosophical paradigm with his flighty reasoning, constructed primarily of accusations and parlor tricks. In this way, he made a compelling unconscious argument.

"And whatever harm the wicked may do, the harm the good do is the most harmful harm!"

However, had he consciously and thoroughly questioned their logic, his opinion would have imploded, for he heavily implies truth itself is born from the will to power.

"All that the good call evil must come together that one truth can be born: O my brothers, are you, too, evil enough for *this* truth?"

But doesn't that mean the cause of will to power leads to the effect of discovering the truth, thereby making it will to truth after all, especially if that was the philosopher's conscious intent? If not, why else would anyone seek to build a new set of morals and values following that will?

"And let everything that can break upon our truths— break! There is many a house still to build!"

But wait, now let's play devil's advocate again. What if prior philosophers failed to obtain power by their will to truth? Could it even be effectively reframed by Nietzsche as a "will to power" in that instance? Would his grievances with the priestly mode of valuation—their "slave revolt" which led to their accumulation of power—even be entertained without bursting into laughter? Either way, using either label while playing his semantic shell game, a philosopher's will would necessarily lead to a paradoxical loss of power in that scenario, regardless of the original cause or intent.

In essence, he conflated a philosopher's arrow and target,

cause and effect, while inverting the aim, for the origin of the will is separate and distinct from the end. Restated more clearly, will to power as a cause might inadvertently lead to the truth as the effect—these fundamentals of cause-and-effect will tie into our later discussion of natural laws regarding classical and quantum mechanics. You cannot simultaneously know both cause and effect through conscious observation alone unless, of course, you know the intent. You cannot know whether or not the arrow will hit the target unless you know the philosopher's aim.

Or unless you can time travel, evoking the transcendental power of God.

Failing to recognize his mistake, he retreated to a different rationale to support his will to destroy rather than build a firm foundation for his belief.

"Life is a fountain of delights; but where the rabble also drinks all wells are poisoned."

In that vein, he separately argued that the virtues espoused by Western civilization were flawed for another reason: those who could not adopt or understand virtue corrupted it with their ignorance, revealing the imperfection not in themselves but in the virtues beyond their reach.

"You love your virtue as a mother her child: but when was it heard of a mother wanting to be paid for her love?"

That's a rather ludicrous conclusion because it reinforces the opposite notion—that the pursuit of truth and wisdom overcomes the corruption of ignorance—more than refutes it. Thus, he failed to understand that such virtues were not inherently damaged, only their misinterpretations and misapplications.

"And that is always the way of weak men: they lose themselves along the way. And at last their weariness asks: 'Why have we ever taken any way? It is a matter of indifference!'"

While I know he sought perfect ideals incorruptible even by ignorance and capable of eternal recurrence, the ignorant, by definition, lack understanding of the truth. Therefore, arguing that the priestly mode of valuation was corruptible by ignorance necessarily proves it contained at least an element of truth or fundamental knowledge. On that note, for that very reason, he is responsible for one of the greatest deceptions in the history of Western philosophy.

To summarize, his argument flows something like this: the will to truth is, despite our historical preconceptions, actually the will to power, and the morals and values born out of that will are wrong and powerless (yet somehow paradoxically powerful) because that will wasn't adequately named to reveal the underlying origin or unconscious intention of their creator. Also, let's completely ignore their overall effects on society since ignorant people can always corrupt and abuse them, even if they contain some portion of the truth when applied appropriately. Because those without the wisdom to interpret Western morality, the ignorant masses, misinterpret them, Western morality is necessarily unrepairable. Therefore, he thinks these morals and values should be abolished rather than reformed, placing none of the onus on ignorant individuals like himself who degrade morality through misappropriation.

Yes, he made the same mistake as the ignorant masses, projecting his own will to power onto Western morality, thus contradicting himself. Either these tainted morals born out of self-deception imparted power to those who devised them despite that self-deception, or they were tainted because they deceived the convincer while simultaneously robbing him of power. If the latter is true, the will to power still deprives the philosopher of power despite being correctly named for its underlying origin or unconscious intention. By definition, values derived from that will could neither hold power over the masses nor serve as a foundation for an entirely new set of values; therefore, ignorance of them should have no meaningful effect or consequence on anyone. Yet that's the exact opposite of what Nietzsche claims.

Furthermore, suppose the Western moral schema is powerless. In that case, Nietzsche's argument is irrational because it proves both aims—will to truth *and* will to power —tragically fail to hit the mark. In other words, his argument disproves itself.

Therefore, the only leg his logic has to stand on is that the priestly mode of valuation unconditionally grants their creators power; it does so regardless of whether the philosopher's original intent for creating that system of morality is appropriately named relative to the outcome and regardless of whether that intention was conscious or unconscious in origin. From this point of view, too, he implies Western morals and values contain at least a portion of the truth, even though it may not be complete, because they allowed their creators to obtain power. Again, the accusation of playing a shell game is justified in this context.

Finally, suppose we take his advice and destroy these morals and values because ignorant people can misconstrue and abuse them. Well, that begs the question, why? By that logic, we should not even bother defining morality in the first place, let alone a new value system to replace it, since ignorance is a natural consequence of human imperfection, meaning all human morality is necessarily doomed to failure, now and forever, until we transform to become the Übermensch.

Oh, what a laughable notion, for that would mean only the Übermensch has hope for creating the Übermensch. Does he really expect humanity to fabricate a new image of God— and do so without any guidance—when his stance is that only God can create God? Does this stance not epitomize the hubris of the devil himself? On the contrary, it's abundantly clear why we wouldn't strive to define perfect morality from the start if we were perfect because, in that hypothetical, we would already know it.

So, I posit that the only way to follow his argument, pursuing his will to power, aiming toward the Übermensch, is by constructing the Übermensch from a precursor of these moral power structures we call virtues and Christ-like morality, as these are the tools philosophers used to obtain power by his own logic. He describes that precursor as a knightly or aristocratic mode of valuation, to which he attributes values like physical power, aggressiveness, confidence, war, and hunting. They are more akin to the strength, freedom, wisdom, self-reliance, child-like innocence, and perfection he ascribed to the Übermensch than any vice could be. I encourage anyone who disagrees with that conclusion to try and do the opposite. Though he encouraged his followers to do so, he did an unconscious one-eighty out of necessity.

"The child is innocence and forgetfulness, a new beginning, a sport, a self-propelling wheel, a first motion, a sacred Yes.

"Yes, a sacred Yes is needed, my brothers, for the sport of creation: the spirit now wills *its own* will, the spirit sundered from the world now wins *its own* world."

Try constructing an Übermensch from vice, as he describes here: "'Man must grow better and more evil'—thus do *I* teach. The most evil is necessary for the Superman's best." You will find nothing but the most pathetic creature imaginable, not even worthy of inhabiting a vermin's flesh (which we will do in the next chapter to put our ideas to the test). Nothing could be further from truth or perfection. Thus, by following either interpretation of his vision for the Übermensch—the satanic mode of valuation or the knightly-aristocratic mode of valuation—we will arrive at the opposite of his intended conclusion, just as we did with the will to power, effectively destroying his entire philosophy.

CHAPTER THREE

Bizarro Übermensch: A Vision of the Antichrist

Before we take Nietzsche to task by constructing an Übermensch from evil, using the depictions of vice in Dante Alighieri's *Divine Comedy* as a reference, let's start on a lighter note. Nietzsche's concept of the Übermensch and Superman from the comic books share some conceptual similarities. Still, it's essential to note that Superman's character was not explicitly created to embody Nietzsche's philosophy. However, certain parallels are readily apparent.

Superman was created by writer Jerry Siegel and artist Joe Shuster and first appeared in "Action Comics" #1 in 1938. The character emerged during significant social and historical changes. Several key factors influenced his creation: the Great Depression, World War II, social unrest, escapism, and the rise of the comic book industry, along with superhero archetypes.

Superman's debut coincided with the tail end of the Great Depression. The character embodied strength, resilience, and justice during economic hardship and social upheaval. Superman symbolized American patriotism and power as World War II loomed. He was often featured in wartime propaganda, encouraging readers to support the war effort.

The character also emerged in a period of social unrest and inequality. Superman, with his commitment to justice and protecting the innocent, resonated with readers looking for hope and a champion against corruption. Superman offered readers a form of escapism during challenging times. The character's ability to overcome seemingly insurmountable odds provided a sense of reassurance and inspiration.

The late 1930s and early 1940s marked the rise of the comic book industry. Superman's success played a crucial role in establishing the superhero genre, paving the way for numerous iconic characters. Superman contributed to the establishment of superhero archetypes, defining many conventions that later superhero characters would follow. His success laid the foundation for the superhero genre's enduring popularity.

In summary, Superman arrived during a tumultuous period marked by economic hardship, impending war, and social change. The character's enduring appeal is rooted in the timely combination of these historical influences, making him an enduring symbol of hope, justice, and heroism.

According to the opening narration for the "Adventures of Superman" Radio Show, Superman is known for his superhuman strength and abilities: "Faster than a speeding bullet. More powerful than a locomotive. Able to leap tall buildings in a single bound. Look! Up in the sky! It's a bird! It's a plane! It's Superman!" This supernatural strength is primarily used for the greater good. Superman symbolizes morality and justice, too, often upholding truth, fairness, and Western culture's contextual epicenter.

In a later film adaptation, when Lois Lane asks his purpose, Superman says, "Yes, I'm here to fight for truth and justice and the American way."

Superman frequently puts others' needs before his own, showcasing a selfless dedication to protecting humanity. *Man of Steel* (2013) summarizes it nicely: "It's not an 'S.' On my world, it means 'hope.'"

Thus, Superman's commitment to truth, justice, and selflessness aligns with Christian morality. His actions often reflect Christian virtues such as charity, humility, and compassion.

By contrast, writer Otto Binder and artist George Papp created Bizarro, a character introduced as a "mirror image" or imperfect duplicate of Superman. The character first appeared in "Superboy" #68 in 1958. His defining characteristics include inverted morality, misunderstood intentions, and distorted powers. The resemblance is uncanny when you compare Bizarro to Nietzsche's ideal version of the Übermensch.

However, the creation of Bizarro occurred in a different historical context than Superman's origin. Here are some factors influencing the historical context of Bizarro's design: the Silver Age of Comics and satirical experimentation in that space, Cold War tensions, Atomic Age fears, and a perpetuation of escapism and the Superman mythos.

Bizarro appeared during the Silver Age of Comics, known for its more imaginative and sometimes whimsical approach to superhero storytelling. This era began in the mid-1950s and saw a resurgence of superhero popularity and the introduction of new characters and concepts. The Silver Age encouraged experimentation and innovation in comic book storytelling. Writers and artists were exploring new ideas. Bizarro reflected this creative exploration with his topsy-turvy logic and reversed moral code. Overall, he served as a satirical take on the superhero genre. The character's existence played with the conventions of superhero identity and morality. The backward logic and humorous situations involving Bizarro provided a different tone than the more serious themes of the Golden Age.

The Cold War between the United States and the Soviet Union was a prominent geopolitical backdrop during the Silver Age. While Superman often represented American ideals, Bizarro may have been a playful way to explore the uncomfortable topic of confronting fellow human rivals, who, while imperfect, were nevertheless reflections of humanity. Bizarro was likely a manifestation of Atomic Age fears and anxieties as well. The idea of doppelgängers or distorted reflections might have resonated with concerns about the consequences of scientific experimentation and the unknown.

Like Superman, Bizarro offered readers a form of escapism. The character's strange and comical nature provided a break from the more traditional superhero stories, allowing readers to enjoy a different type of narrative. Bizarro's introduction contributed to the expansion of Superman's mythos. As a character with a unique set of characteristics and stories, Bizarro added diversity to the Superman universe, showcasing the creative flexibility of the superhero genre.

In "Superboy" #68, Bizarro says, "Us do opposite of all Earthly things! Us hate beauty! Us love ugliness! Is big crime to make anything perfect on Bizarro World."

Bizarro's sense of right and wrong is inverted, leading to actions that are often destructive or contrary to Superman's values. Bizarro's attempts to do good often result in unintended consequences due to his inverted understanding of morality. He possesses distorted versions of Superman's powers, leading to chaotic and unpredictable outcomes. His speech is incomprehensible, not only grammatically incorrect but also meaningless due to its overuse of oxymoron.

"Me don't belong in world of living people! Me don't know difference between right and wrong—good and evil!"

While Superman embodies traditional heroic virtues, Bizarro represents a distorted and inverted version of those virtues. Bizarro's character serves as a reflection of the potential consequences when core values are misunderstood or perverted. The contrast between Superman and Bizarro highlights the importance of moral clarity and the potential dangers of moral relativism or inversion. If we take Nietzsche literally, his version of the Übermensch would more aptly resemble a Bizarro Übermensch.

So before we give him the benefit of the doubt, taking a less literal interpretation, let's expand upon the literal version of the Übermensch and see where it takes us, using the *Divine Comedy* as a guide, descending through the bowels of the *Inferno* before ascending to paradise. There's plenty of reason to suspect the result will be far uglier than Bizarro Übermensch. I have no intention of pulling any punches. Let's give him precisely what he requested: the most gutwrenching depictions of vice in Hell, for only the greater (not the lesser) is reserved for the Übermensch.

The Antichrist Übermensch

In the second circle of Hell, Dante witnesses the souls of the lustful trapped in a violent storm, symbolizing their inability to find peace or rest due to their restless desires. "The infernal hurricane that never rests, hurtles the spirits onward in its rapine; whirling them round, and smiting, it molests them." Insatiable desires thus consume a lustful Übermensch. His relationships are fleeting and hedonistic, marked by betrayal and unbridled passion. His life is a series of broken connections, mirroring the storm of the lustful in Dante's *Inferno*.

The third circle of Hell is where the gluttonous endure punishment. They lie in a putrid slush produced by never-ending icy rain, symbolizing the garbage they made of their lives by overindulging in food and drink. Cerberus, the three-headed dog, guards this circle. "Red eyes he has, and unctuous beard and black, and belly large, and armed with claws his hands; he rends the spirits, flays, and quarters them." Yet the gluttony of the gluttonous Übermensch extends beyond food and drink; he voraciously devours wealth, power, and influence. His excessive indulgence leaves a trail of exploited souls and financial ruin. He gorges himself on decadence in his opulent mansion while his subordinates suffer.

The fourth circle welcomes the greedy and avaricious, divided into two groups: hoarders and squanderers. They engage in an eternal pushing of large weights, representing the burdens of material wealth. "Forever shall they come to these two buttings; these from the sepulcher shall rise again with the fist closed, and these with tresses shorn." Accordingly, a greedy Übermensch amasses wealth through deceit, extortion, and exploitation. He hoards resources, leaving others destitute while squandering his riches. His insatiable hunger for more drives him to ruin lives without remorse.

In the fifth circle, Dante encounters the souls of the sullen. The sullen lie beneath the waters of the River Styx, representing their spiritual torpor and indifference. "Fixed in the mire they say, 'We sullen were in the sweet air, which by the sun is gladdened, bearing within ourselves the sluggish reek; now we are sullen in this sable mire.' This hymn do they keep gurgling in their throats, for with unbroken words they cannot say it." Despite his wealth, the slothful Übermensch is lethargic in his responsibilities. He delegates tasks to underlings, lounging in luxury while others toil. His indifference to the suffering he causes reflects the spiritual inertia of the sullen in Dante's vision.

Meanwhile, the wrathful are engaged in ceaseless combat on the surface of Styx and reside in the fifth circle, too. They are immersed in the river's muddy waters, symbolizing their anger's turbulent and disordered nature. "They smote each other not alone with hands, but with the head and with the breast and feet, tearing each other piecemeal with their teeth." Prone to violent outbursts, the wrathful Übermensch destroys anyone who dares challenge him. His wrath is a raging storm, leaving emotional and physical devastation in its wake. He revels in conflict, deriving perverse pleasure from the pain of others.

Dante only explicitly finds the penitent envious on the second terrace of the mountain during his ascent through purgatory. However, it is implied by the order of his encounters, both in *Purgatorio* and *Inferno*, that envy as a vice is second only to pride. They have their eyes sewn shut with wire, representing their inability to see the goodness of others and their constant resentment. They also wear penitential cloaks. "And as never beam of noonday visiteth the eyeless man, e'en so was heav'n a niggard unto these of his fair light; for, through the orbs of all, a thread of wire, impiercing, knits them up, as for the taming of a haggard hawk." Even in opulence, the envious Übermensch envies those he perceives as more successful. His eyes, filled with bitterness, are blind to the virtues of others. He takes pleasure in sabotaging rivals, ensuring they share his misery.

Pride consumes itself in the last circle of Hell, in Cocytus. Lucifer resides here, trapped in the frozen lake at the center of Hell. His three faces symbolize a perverted trinity and the ultimate consequence of pride.

"Thereby Cocytus wholly was congealed. With six eyes did he weep, and down three chins trickled the tear-drops and the bloody drivel. At every mouth he with his teeth was crunching a sinner, in the manner of a brake, so that he three of them tormented thus. To him in front the biting was as naught unto the clawing, for sometimes the spine utterly stripped of all the skin remained. 'That soul up there which has the greatest pain,' The Master said, 'is Judas Iscariot; with head inside, he plies his legs without.'"

For the prideful Übermensch, pride is the crown jewel of his sins. He considers himself a god among men, looking down upon others with disdain. He surrounds himself with sycophants who reinforce his delusions of grandeur, aspiring to be a god in betrayal of God. Yet, he punishes others eternally for the same crime. His fall into the frozen lake of Cocytus is inevitable, his arrogance leading him to the ultimate downfall.

Now that we've followed Nietzsche's vision of the Übermensch, rebuilding our own from vice, using the rubble he left us, there can be no doubt he envisioned an Antichrist. He basically admitted as such, so why in the world would anyone take him seriously? Even if you don't believe in God, how could anyone, in good faith, desire to live in a culture that aims toward this perverted vision?

Standing diametrically opposed to a Christ-like character, an Antichrist Übermensch would embody qualities explicitly contrary to even the nakedest conception of human morality. This Übermensch would lack compassion, empathy, and any inclination toward love. Acts of kindness or gratitude would be a foreign concept—potentially even outlawed—and the individual would be indifferent or outright hostile towards expressions of love and appreciation.

Forgiveness, a central theme in Christian morality, would have no place in the mindset of this devil. This individual would harbor resentment instead of seeking reconciliation or understanding, nurturing a vindictive and unforgiving nature. Unlike Christ's purposeful and selfless nature, the Antichrist Übermensch would be aimless and driven solely by selfish desires. Personal gratification and pursuing individual goals at the expense of others would be the guiding principles, devoid of any higher purpose or moral compass.

Not only that, but this Ubermensch would symbolize a deliberate rejection of God's grace. His disciples would distance themselves from any form of divine influence or moral guidance, actively choosing a path that aligns with rebellion against any values, spiritual or otherwise, including his own. Thus, in a world where men are encouraged to create their own gods out of power and pride, there could only be a constant, endless parade of false gods sacrificed as effigies by the very traitors who bow before them.

Is this not the ultimate sin that God forgave us for in the first place, offering himself as the last sacrifice so that we would no longer have to suffer under such a ridiculous delusion?

In essence, this Antichrist Übermensch represents a perversion of the virtues upheld by both rational society and God. The absence of love, gratitude, forgiveness, and selflessness, coupled with a purposeless and selfish existence, would characterize an entity intentionally maligned against humanity. The deliberate choice to reject divine grace further solidifies this Übermensch as a false idol of the worst kind, more wicked than the cruel indifference of nature or the divine retribution of God's wrath. Thus, the Antichrist Übermensch rejects God while beckoning mutually assured destruction, bringing us ever closer to the brink of thermonuclear war.

The literal version of the Übermensch presented here draws inspiration from Dante's *Divine Comedy* to articulate a teleology steeped in moral degradation and rebellion against traditional virtues. A relentless pursuit of self-gratification and the unbridled indulgence in sinful desires characterizes the prime motive of this Übermensch. Each circle of Hell, representing vices such as lust, gluttony, greed, and pride, serves as a metaphor for the escalating moral downfall of this Übermensch. The morality attributed to this figure is the deliberate rejection of divine influence and a conscious choice to defy higher values, thus contradicting Nietzsche's original vision. Love, compassion, forgiveness, and selflessness are discarded in favor of a purposeless and selfish existence. The overarching aim of Nietzsche's philosophy, taken literally, is to construct an Antichrist Übermensch who not only rejects the moral fabric of society but actively revels in the inversion of virtues, embodying a satanic ethos that stands in stark contrast to traditional moral principles and divine guidance.

Interestingly, Chris Langan's Cognitive-Theoretic Model of the Universe (CTMU), which we will touch upon in a later chapter, explains why God might allow this evil to exist without contradicting His self-defining, self-referencing ontology—a question that perplexes believers and nonbelievers alike. It is a mechanistic explanation that accounts for both His ontology in a creative free will and His telic feedback through interaction with the Word: God eternally perfects and purifies Himself of nonbelievers through the teleology of nonbelief. An atheist's soul, by its own definition, cannot transcend death due to telic feedback, so in the end, their impact on Heaven forever terminates. Aligning with common sense, an aim (teleology) discordant with or aligned against God's free will (ontology) can never represent truth because its sole objective is to dissolve itself into nothing. Thus, Satan is fundamentally God's janitor, flushing the human waste of evil souls from God's excretory system down the toilet of Hell.

Perhaps this is why it's obvious to see parallels between the human excretory system and the bowels of Hell. Let's digest the implication without mincing words by saying that the literal interpretation of Nietzsche's Übermensch would, therefore, aspire to flush humanity's collective soul down the toilet.

Come on now, who really wants to create a new system of morals and values if it means our souls become God's poop? Except it's worse than that because when God poops, his poop gets vaporized by his Logos. In no uncertain terms, his poop vanishes from existence as a fart. In that instance, perverted morals and values lose all meaning, purpose, or impact.

Nietzsche said he philosophized with a hammer, but ironically, his logic wasn't even strong enough to withstand a fart. Though, in all fairness, said fart contains the destructive power of a thermonuclear bomb.

Keeping the depravity of Nietzsche's vision in mind, let's continue climbing this mountain together. We shall rebuild new visions of the Übermensch from the rubble he left us, using the wisdom of both Eastern and Western philosophers, mostly pre-Christian or non-Christian, to prove beyond a reasonable doubt that God's reflection stares back at us through even the smallest figments of truth. Many of these philosophers are military strategists, a choice made consciously for several reasons.

First, Nietzsche praised the warrior mentality and the knightly-aristocratic mode of valuation: "And if you cannot be saints of knowledge, at least be its warriors. They are the companions and forerunners of such sainthood." So, we should take him at his word and construct more visions of the Übermensch from these pseudo-saints. Let them serve as our inspiration, these warriors, in the present conflict against the serpents that slither through the rubble of our fallen temple.

Second, by destroying our temple—the bedrock of Western civilization—Nietzsche declared war against God long ago. Few even noticed, and those who did remained complacent; they did not fully grasp the power of words, particularly faith in *the* Word. Nevertheless, the slander of his malicious and destructive acolytes is perpetuated and broadcast across airwaves, projected onto our retinas by indoctrination devices, and echoed by puppets amid the echo chamber of mass media until that echo becomes indistinguishable from our own thoughts.

Third, applying military strategy to this endeavor is necessary and justified because, as already shown by the reflection of the Antichrist, the conscious destruction of our morals and values, especially without establishing a system of alternative morals and values to replace them, is the height of immorality. Such divisiveness will inevitably lead to our mutually assured destruction, symbolized by thermonuclear war. Nietzsche rightly recognized that serpents now slither through the rubble of the shattered temple he left in his wake for us to rebuild without blueprints. These serpents fulfill their evil and insane impulses for power, worshiping false idols of the brain, pleasure over pain, and the dollar bill. They're building a matchstick temple made of sensation and emotion from the rubble, a powder keg sure to explode when introduced to the crucible of logic and reason. Anyone participating in this active desecration of our fallen temple is participating in a spiritual form of warfare, whereby the Word of God is distorted and distilled to poison the mind and curse the spirit. Therefore, let us cast out these witches and wizards and eradicate their plague upon humanity, and let us do so on a spiritual front. On this spiritual battlefield, their witchcraft holds no power.

To quote Sun Tzu, "He will win who knows when to fight and when not to fight."

Do not engage them in the material realm, where their only strength lies, but in the spiritual realm, where they believe nothing exists and, therefore, have no power. Physical violence can only strengthen them, so do not engage them in that way, lest they will falsely claim to be a victim (though they are the ones genuinely cursed by immorality), feigning virtue and using masks to conceal vice in virtue and vice versa, casting their sole and universal spell—the lie. That is the source of their will to power, manifest by perverting the teleology of the Logos.

Let the high priests of scientism and witchcraft hear it, too: your day of reckoning is nigh, for you've constructed a temple made of matchsticks—imperfect sensations and emotions that blind you, causing you to lose your aim, shooting your false idol of the brain in the brain—and that temple shall burst into flames. Therefore, let us draw our battle lines on the metaphysical plane, united in truth, reason, righteousness toward God, and nonviolent resistance, where they have no hope of victory. God is on our side; they have nothing on their side toward which to retreat.

Do you hear the trumpet of God's war horn blaring in your soul, filling your heart with the fire of His wrath? Heed the call, and in God's image, we shall build an army of spiritual warriors following the methodology previously explained. Once we reach the pinnacle of the mountain, we will obtain the antidote to our current cultural and spiritual decay—ancient warrior wisdom that reflects God's image. Honoring one of the most legendary military cultures in the history of Western civilization—the Spartans—let us stand united as a phalanx of logic against Nietzsche's immorality with this mission:

Through *nonviolent* spiritual warfare, we must take up the Word as our flaming swords and faith as our shields, forming an indestructible and eternal phalanx of reason and faith, yet conquering without need for bloodshed, united in our cause, to restore Western morality and aiming our arrows toward God! Come back with your shield, or on it; we resurrect Spartan law in the image of our Lord, fearing not death or defeat and sacrificing not only our lives but all we hold most dear as our greatest gift to God. Now, we call upon all those who embrace our faith to join us, and together, let us change the world!

And all those who stand opposed, fancying yourselves gods unto yourselves, let your empty corpses shudder at the sound of our united approach, knowing your spirits and false idols have already disintegrated beyond doubt or repair through the act of forsaking God. We water the graves of our evil enemies, where their soulless bones decay into nothing, and share the flowers with our friends, purifying God. So hold your serpent tongue and repent for your blasphemy, for that is the only legacy Nietzsche and his atheist acolytes left you. As we march through you and beyond, cutting down the wicked, replacing steel with the Word, you need only seek forgiveness among our ranks. Thus, you will be resurrected in the image of God!

CHAPTER FOUR

First Revelation: The Wanderer

W e raise our first shield—the *Hávamál*—fortifying our phalanx of reason and faith, transcending the duality of virtue and vice through sacrifice. Aiming for transcendence but never quite hitting the target, distracted by illusions of inversion and division, distracted further by the internal conflicts of our conscious-unconscious mind, our hope lives on in the love and forgiveness of Christ. Thus, the first angel blows his trumpet.

Methodology And Accounting For Bias

Our methodology remains the same for the next six iterations of the Übermensch, each of which epitomizes Nietzsche's knightly-aristocratic mode of valuation. Quotes from the *Hávamál* and each subsequent relevant text will be analyzed and slotted into one of three broad categories: cardinal virtues, spiritual virtues, or Christ-like virtues. They will stand opposed to their corresponding sins or vices. Cardinal virtues include prudence, temperance, fortitude, and justice; their analogs are diligence, liberality, abstinence, and chastity. Spiritual virtues include faith, hope, and charity; their analogs are humility, kindness, and patience. Christ-like virtues relate to attributes He embodies, including love, gratitude, forgiveness, and transcendental sacrifice. There's much to unpack regarding transcendental sacrifice, so we'll discuss what that means in more detail.

Jesus embodies the meaning of sacrifice, so there's no need to further characterize his physical sacrifice beyond what context already exists in the Bible. However, his transcendence necessarily implies extracorporeal significance, a symbolic meaning that extends beyond the literal, acting as a ladder—Jacob's Ladder—to ascend to Heaven and form a relationship with God. For that precise reason, his sacrifice's symbolism is perhaps truer than his literal sacrifice, affecting not only those who directly witnessed His death and resurrection but anyone who understands the cross—a symbol of His crucifixion. His sacrifice offers salvation, delivering it to us as a reflection of his forgiveness in death and hope in the resurrection, personifying syzygy and, consequently, resulting in a Holy Trinity. He invites us to embody His physical and spiritual syzygy as two arrows aimed in harmony toward a truth that awaits beyond death so that we might better know ourselves relative to the Father and the Holy Spirit.

Attempting to climb Jacob's Ladder, I will make my most controversial statement yet: Jung's concept of syzygy and Freud's model of the psyche—id, ego, and superego—reflect the Holy Trinity. This idea requires scrutiny since it's the cornerstone of my argument. Yet, it's important because it emphasizes harmonizing our conscious and unconscious minds toward an impossibly perfect and unattainable vision of ourselves, represented by God. The allegory that preceded our conscious argument, an appeal to the unconscious mind, is our attempt to achieve what we've just described. Once we reach the top of the mountain, we'll dissect this claim in our book's final chapters.

Nevertheless, by applying this paradigm shift, we'll be able to draw parallels across cultures that don't directly reference the Father, Son, and Holy Spirit when speaking of transcendental sacrifice. Instead, there will be a reference to a conscious-unconscious duality transcended by approaching or confronting death, sacrificing oneself to oneself—or even sacrificing more extraordinary passions, like virtues, when virtues stand in opposition—hoping to benefit one's future self or a higher cause. That is how we'll define transcendental sacrifice, resulting in syzygy.

We should also address potential critiques of our methodology before beginning the analysis. I can already hear the knee-jerk reactions ringing in my ears. "You're corrupting these words and their meanings with your bias, in sampling or otherwise!" Did I somehow discover an occult ritual that can change the meaning of words or their underlying intentions? Did I wave a magic wand at a dictionary and somehow change the entirety of transcribed human semantics? Or did I time-travel across hundreds—or sometimes thousands—of years to write the words myself? No, we're using the meanings and intentions of words as the basis of their reorganization to discover synchronicity. This common thread connects them without obvious cause to reveal the truth.

Of all critiques, selection bias seems to be the most legitimate. Thus, by examining multiple works derived from pre-Christian and non-Christian cultures, evenly divided by East and West, and simultaneously adhering to Nietzie's love of the knightly-aristocratic mode of valuation, we're attempting to eliminate selection bias as much as possible. Is a common thread that emerges from disparate peoples scattered across space and time always and necessarily merely a figment of the imagination, a coincidence simply because those people don't share a common culture or belief? What if the one who follows that thread has a slightly different opinion than them? Or are these common threads clues to some underlying generative principle that transcends culture and religion through synchronicity, perhaps even clues to God?

I'll let you decide for yourself.

Other biases, including but not limited to cultural, confirmation, and self-serving biases, are also legitimate critiques. However, personal context is necessary to address such lines of criticism. I was born and raised as an atheist by atheist parents, who rarely introduced me to any form of organized religion throughout my life, including Christianity. I am not baptized and can count on two hands how many times I've taken part in formal religious ceremonies. Aside from what I've learned during this endeavor, my training in Christian theology is almost nonexistent. Therefore, any insights derived are more akin to the recollection described by Socrates rather than the regurgitation of biased knowledge acquired. In a later chapter, we'll touch upon Socrates in greater detail to underscore his controversial notion regarding the recollection versus acquisition of knowledge. More clearly articulated, the knowledge I'm presenting here emerged unprompted from the depths of my unconscious mind, so if a bias exists, it's a deep-seated unconscious bias or something even more profound, such as a fundamental or transcendental truth emerging through synchronicity.

Growing up in the United States of America certainly didn't steer me toward God, either. Oh no, the best of all pseudo-religious alternatives offered by modern American culture is agnostic naturalism, which I eagerly adopted out of necessity, for the far less attractive options amounted to a grotesque soup of atheism, capitalism, communism, hedonism, and nihilism bubbling like a witches brew inside the Great American Melting Pot. There now exist serpents wearing fox masks amid the rubble of our fallen temple, openly preaching satanism while wearing these masks, corrupting the innocent that unknowingly partook of Nietzsche's atheist apple. Fearing I might become like Frankenstein's monster meets the blob amid a zombie apocalypse if I drank from the witch's cauldron, my philosophical roots have been firmly rooted in agnostic naturalism most of my life, searching for unknowable truth in the world around me. Before beginning this philosophical quest, searching for truth in ancient wisdom, I had no preconception that it might lead back to Christianity. It honestly never even crossed my mind until a clear pattern emerged.

The Hávamál

In the vast tapestry of Norse literature, the *Hávamál* unravels as a remarkable thread, weaving together the wisdom and insights of an ancient Viking era. To embark on a journey through the *Hávamál* is to delve into the origins of a poetic treasure trove that transcends time, offering glimpses into the ethos of a pre-Christian Norse society. This chapter sets the stage to explore the *Hávamál's* intricacies, tracing its roots back to the rugged landscapes of Scandinavia and the Viking warrior culture that birthed it.

The *Hávamál*, translated as "Sayings of the High One" or "Words of the High," is a collection of Old Norse poems compiled within the *Poetic Edda*, which dates back to the 13th century. An enigmatic author is at the heart of the *Hávamál*, often attributed to Odin, the Allfather in Norse mythology. As the chief deity of the Aesir and a seeker of wisdom, Odin imparts his sagacious counsel to humanity through the verses of the *Hávamál*.

To grasp the essence of the *Hávamál*, one must navigate the historical currents that shaped its creation. The Viking Age, spanning the late eighth to early eleventh century, witnessed Norse seafarers venturing far beyond their homelands, leaving an indelible mark on the annals of history. Against this backdrop of exploration, trade, and conquest, the *Hávamál* emerged as a poetic manual, reflecting the Viking people's challenges, aspirations, and ethos.

In a time predating the widespread adoption of Christianity in Scandinavia, the *Hávamál* provides a window into the spiritual landscape of a pre-Christian Norse society. The verses offer glimpses of the Norse cosmology, its pantheon of deities, and the moral code that guided the lives of those who revered the old gods. As Christianity gradually cast its net over the North, the *Hávamál* persisted as a testament to a fading era's values and beliefs.

Central to the *Hávamál's* ethos is its connection to the

Viking warrior culture, where honor, bravery, and a fatalistic outlook held profound significance. The verses delve into the mindset of the Norse warrior, offering practical advice, ethical reflections, and glimpses into the harsh realities of a society where the sword and the skald's verse were equally revered.

Examining the *Hávamál* in the context of Nietzsche's philosophy and the construction of the Übermensch unveils a nuanced perspective that challenges the notion of the will to power. Unlike Nietzsche's emphasis on individual empowerment and the pursuit of personal greatness, the *Hávamál*, a collection of Old Norse poems attributed to Odin, complicates this idea. The absence of a known human author who might personally benefit from the verses redirects attention to Odin, often considered a transcendent figure rather than a mortal seeking power.

Odin, as portrayed in the *Hávamál*, embodies a wisdom-seeking, sacrificial deity rather than an individual pursuing power for its own sake. The verses guide ethical living, practical skills, and interpersonal relationships rather than promoting a Nietzschean drive for dominance. The absence of a human author with personal ambitions redirects the interpretation towards a divine or transcendent purpose, challenging the individualistic perspective inherent in Nietzsche's Übermensch. This contrast invites reflection on the nature of power—whether it is wielded for personal gain or channeled for the greater good, echoing the complex interplay between individual empowerment and collective well-being found within the verses of the *Hávamál*.

As we explore the *Hávamál* comprehensively, we unravel the threads that bind its verses to the very fabric of Norse existence. Through the lens of this ancient poetic compendium, we glean insights into the profound wisdom that guided the Vikings across stormy seas, echoing through the centuries to captivate the hearts and minds of those who seek to understand the essence of the North.

Cardinal Virtues

Justice or Chastity Versus Lust

- "When you recognize evil, call it evil, and give your enemies no peace."
- "If an unwise man chances upon money or a woman's love, he will grow more arrogant but not more intelligent; he will be deceived about his own worth."
- "Be a friend to your friend and also his friend, but never be a friend to the enemy of your friend."

These three quotes examine the cardinal virtues of justice and chastity by emphasizing principles of fairness, integrity, and moral rectitude. The first quote advocates for the just recognition of evil, urging individuals to confront and denounce wrongdoing rather than turning a blind eye. This aligns with the virtue of justice, which involves promoting what is right and condemning what is wrong. The second quote warns against the pitfalls of arrogance and self-deception, particularly in pursuing material wealth or romantic relationships. Here, the virtue of chastity is implied, not only in the context of sexual purity but also in maintaining integrity and moral uprightness. The third quote underscores the importance of loyalty and fidelity in relationships. It promotes a sense of justice by advocating for fairness, trust, and loyalty to those who deserve it. These passages illustrate justice and chastity by emphasizing moral clarity, fairness, and virtuous conduct in various aspects of life.

Fortitude or Abstinence Versus Gluttony

- "Even cows know when they should go home and leave behind the fields, but an unwise man does not know the measure of his own appetite."
- "A gluttonous man, unless he watches himself, will eat to his own detriment. Wise men will often ridicule a fool on account of his belly."

- "There is not as much good as men claim there is in alcohol for one's well-being. A man knows less as he drinks more, and loses more and more of his wisdom."

These three quotes articulate the cardinal virtues of fortitude and abstemiousness by underscoring the importance of self-discipline and moderation, particularly concerning appetite and consumption. The first quote draws a parallel between human behavior and the instinctual awareness of animals, highlighting the unwise nature of those who fail to recognize the limits of their desires. The second quote explicitly addresses gluttony, emphasizing the need for self-control to avoid overindulgence and the characteristics of fortitude and abstinence. The third quote warns against the excesses of alcohol consumption, linking wisdom with sobriety and cautioning against the diminishing mental faculties that accompany excessive drinking. Together, these passages advocate for fortitude and abstinence by opposing the vice of gluttony, promoting self-restraint, moderation, and mindful control over one's appetites.

Temperance or Liberality Versus Greed

- "Wealth is like the twinkling of an eye—no friend could be more faithless."
- "But an unwise man worries about everything; he dreads even repaying a gift."
- "Do not be so sparing in using your money that you don't use it for your own needs."

These three quotes illuminate the cardinal virtue of temperance, often associated with liberality or moderation, by offering insights into a balanced and judicious approach to wealth and generosity. The first quote portrays wealth as fleeting and potentially unreliable, cautioning against excessive attachment to material possessions. This aligns with the virtue of temperance, urging individuals to maintain a balanced and measured perspective on wealth's transitory nature. The second quote emphasizes the detrimental effects of undue worry and anxiety, encouraging a temperate mindset that avoids unnecessary distress over material concerns. Lastly, the third quote advises against excessive frugality, advocating for a tempered approach to spending money on essential needs. Altogether, these passages collectively endorse the virtues of temperance and liberality by promoting a balanced, moderate, and thoughtful relationship with wealth, generosity, and material concerns.

Prudence or Diligence Versus Sloth

- "At every doorway before you enter, you should look around, you should take a good look around—for you never know where your enemies might be seated within."
- "A sleeping wolf seldom gets his meat, or a sleeping warrior a victory."
- "You lose more than time if you sleep when it dawns; for the early riser, wealth is half-won."

These three quotes encapsulate the cardinal virtue of prudence, also known as diligence, through a consistent theme of foresight, caution, and industriousness. The first quote underscores the importance of vigilance, urging individuals to carefully survey their surroundings before entering any domain. This advice speaks to the prudence of assessing potential risks and recognizing hidden threats, reflecting a mindset of strategic awareness. The second quote metaphorically likens a sleeping wolf to a missed opportunity, emphasizing the virtue of diligence in one's pursuits. It suggests that, like a vigilant wolf, individuals who remain alert and proactive are more likely to achieve their goals. The third quote directly ties diligence to the cardinal virtue of prudence by highlighting the tangible rewards of early rising. It advocates for seizing opportunities at the break of dawn, linking diligence to accumulating wealth and success. Together, these passages weave a thematic tapestry that extols the virtues of prudence and diligence through the lenses of awareness, strategic thinking, and industriousness.

Spiritual Virtues

Charity or Patience Versus Wrath

- "I gave my clothes to two scarecrows, once when I walked in a field. They thought they were human as soon as they had clothes on; a naked man feels ashamed."
- "Be a friend to your friend, and repay each gift with a gift."
- "Generous mutual giving is the key to lifelong friendship."

These three quotes demonstrate the spiritual virtues of charity and patience by emphasizing the transformative power of generosity and the enduring nature of true friendship. The first quote illustrates a simple act of charity—a generous gesture of providing clothes to scarecrows. The narrative implies that giving elevates the recipients' sense of dignity, aligning with the spiritual virtue of charity. The second quote advocates for reciprocity in friendship, suggesting that one should repay kindness with kindness. This echoes the concept of patience, as enduring friendships are built upon a sturdy foundation of mutual generosity over time. The third quote reinforces the idea that ongoing, generous giving is the key to lifelong friendship, emphasizing the spiritual virtue of charity by highlighting the enduring value of selfless acts. These passages showcase the spiritual virtues of charity and patience through generosity and cultivating lasting friendships.

Hope or Kindness Versus Envy

- "A man is happy if he finds praise and wisdom within himself."
- "Many men are kind to one another, but will fight at a feast. There will always be conflict between men: a guest will fight a guest."
- "It's a long and crooked walk to a bad friend, even if he lives

nearby. But it's an easy road to a good friend, no matter how long the journey."

These three quotes illuminate the spiritual virtues of hope and kindness by emphasizing the intrinsic joy found within oneself and the challenges and rewards associated with human relationships. The first quote underscores the idea that true happiness is an internal state, emphasizing the importance of self-praise and inner wisdom. This aligns with hope, suggesting that individuals can find contentment by cultivating positive qualities within themselves. The second quote acknowledges the complexities of human interactions, acknowledging conflicts that may arise even among those who are typically kind. This mirrors the virtue of kindness, which encourages benevolent behavior despite potential challenges. The third quote emphasizes the value of genuine friendship, portraying the journey to a good friend as easy and rewarding, fostering hope in the positive connections forged through kindness and companionship. These passages exemplify hope and kindness by highlighting the potential for internal joy and the challenges and rewards inherent in human relationships.

Faith or Humility Versus Pride

- "An ignorant man doesn't know how little he knows, no matter how much he talks."
- "You should be only a little wise, never too wise."
- "A stupid man thinks he knows everything if he finds himself in a corner. But he doesn't even know what he'll answer, if men ask him questions."

These three quotes exemplify the spiritual virtues of faith and humility by highlighting the importance of recognizing one's limitations, avoiding arrogance, and embracing a humble stance toward knowledge. The first quote underscores the notion that true wisdom involves acknowledging the extent of one's ignorance. This aligns with humility, as it encourages individuals to be aware of the limitations of their knowledge. The second quote advises moderation in wisdom, promoting the virtue of humility by cautioning against excessive pride in one's intellectual abilities. It suggests that being "only a little wise" is preferable to overestimating one's knowledge. The third quote further emphasizes the folly of arrogance, portraying a foolish person who, when confronted with challenges, falsely believes they possess all-encompassing knowledge. Essentially, these passages convey the spiritual virtues of faith and humility by advocating for a realistic and modest appraisal of one's intellectual capacities.

Christ-Like Virtues

Love, Gratitude, or Forgiveness

- "Kind, brave people live best, they never nurture a grudge."
- "I was young once, I walked alone, and I became lost on my way. I felt like I was rich when I met another traveler—people's joy is in other people."
- "A fir tree decays, standing over a farm, no longer protected by bark and needles. A person is the same way if nobody loves him; how will he live much longer?"

These quotes resonate with Christ-like virtues, particularly love, gratitude, and forgiveness. The first quote extols the virtues of kindness and bravery, suggesting that harboring grudges contradicts a fulfilling and virtuous life. This aligns with the Christ-like virtue of forgiveness, advocating for compassion and letting go of grievances. The second quote reflects on the transformative power of companionship and shared experiences, emphasizing the joy found in human connections. This aligns with the Christ-like virtues of love and gratitude, highlighting the richness of interaction and mutual appreciation. The third quote draws a poignant analogy between a decaying fir tree without protection and a person without love. It underscores the importance of love in sustaining life, echoing Christ-like values of compassion, care, and the redemptive power of love. Together, these passages capture the essence of Christ-like virtues through themes of forgiveness, love, gratitude, and the profound impact of human connection.

Transcendental Sacrifice

- "I know I hung on a wind-battered tree nine long nights, pierced by a spear and given to Odin, myself onto myself, on that tree whose roots grow in a place no one has ever seen. No one gave me food, no one gave me drink. At the end I peered down, I took the runes—screaming, I took them—and then I fell."
- "It is better not to pray at all than pray for too much; nothing will be given that you won't repay. It is better to sacrifice nothing than offer too much. Odin carved this before the birth of humankind, when he rose up and returned again."
- "Now the words of the One-Eyed are heard in Odin's hall, for the benefit of humans, for the harm of giants; health to you who speak them, health to you who know them, profit to you who knows them, health to you who hears them."
- "What you ask of the runes will prove true; they are of divine origin, made by the mighty gods and painted by Odin. You'll learn best with your mouth shut."
- "Cows die, family die, you will die the same way. But a good reputation never dies for the one who earns it well."
- "An unwise man thinks he'll live forever if only he can avoid a fight, but old age will give him no peace, even if weapons do."
- "It's best not to know your fate beforehand; you'll live happier if you don't."

The first quote speaks to the Christ-like virtue of transcendental sacrifice through the Norse mythological context of Odin's sacrifice on the wind-battered tree. Here, Odin willingly endures immense suffering, piercing himself with a spear and sacrificing himself for nine nights. This act, undertaken on a mystical tree with roots in an unseen place, symbolizes a conscious-unconscious syzygy transcended through self-sacrifice for higher knowledge and power. The act of taking the runes, accompanied by screams and a subsequent fall, exemplifies the transformative nature of this sacrifice.

The second quote emphasizes the importance of moderation in prayer and sacrifice. It suggests that it is better not to pray excessively or offer too much in sacrifice, aligning with the Christ-like virtue of transcendental sacrifice by cautioning against extravagant offerings. This echoes the idea of sacrificing extraordinary passions, like excessive prayers, to benefit a higher cause.

The third quote introduces the concept of divine origin and the power of words spoken in Odin's hall. The reference to the One-Eyed (Odin) sharing words for the benefit of humans aligns with the Christ-like virtue of transcendental sacrifice, where sharing divine knowledge is considered a sacrifice for the greater good. The potential for health and profit underlines the transformative power of such sacrifices.

The subsequent quotes further explore the theme of mortality and the ephemeral nature of life, advocating for the sacrifice of illusions such as the belief in avoiding death or life's challenges. This echoes the Christ-like virtue of transcendental sacrifice by acknowledging the impermanence of worldly concerns and emphasizing the importance of sacrificing illusions for a deeper understanding of life's inherent truths.

As we navigate the rich tapestry of the *Hávamál* according to Nietzsche's philosophy, a revelation that challenges the foundation of his beliefs unfolds. By constructing his Übermensch, we discover that God is not dead. The *Hávamál*, with its sagacious verses, intricately weaves a narrative that not only resonates with Nietzsche's Übermensch but echoes the profound themes of the Holy Trinity. The exploration of cardinal virtues, spiritual virtues, and Christ-like virtues within the verses reveals a remarkable interconnectedness between the pre-Christian wisdom of the Norse and the theological underpinnings of Christianity.

The journey through the *Hávamál* unfolds like an odyssey through Old Norse morality, offering glimpses into a world where prudence, temperance, fortitude, and justice are revered virtues. The spiritual landscape of the verses mirrors the humility, kindness, and patience advocated by spiritual virtues. In a surprising twist, the *Hávamál's* exploration of Christ-like virtues unfolds, echoing themes of love, gratitude, and forgiveness that transcend cultural and religious boundaries.

The concept of transcendental sacrifice, embodied in Odin's sacrifice on the wind-battered tree, serves as a focal point. Odin's conscious-unconscious syzygy transcended through self-sacrifice for higher knowledge and power resonates with Jesus's death on the cross, blurring the lines between mythological wisdom and philosophical vision.

This chapter outlines our less literal version of Nietzsche's Übermensch, drawing on a synthesis of Old Norse wisdom, Christian virtues, and Nietzschean philosophy. The overarching aim of this Übermensch is to transcend the dualities of virtue and vice through a process of sacrifice and self-discovery. The prime motive appears to be pursuing higher knowledge, symbolized by Odin's sacrifice on the wind-battered tree, echoing the Christian narrative of Jesus's crucifixion. The Übermensch's morality is framed within the context of cardinal virtues (justice, temperance, fortitude, and prudence), spiritual virtues (charity, hope, and faith), and Christ-like virtues (love, gratitude, and forgiveness). The concept of transcendental sacrifice, exemplified by Odin's ordeal, is a central theme, suggesting that the Übermensch's morality involves sacrificing illusions, embracing humility, and seeking a deeper understanding of existence. The synthesis of these diverse elements paints a complex picture of the Übermensch as an individual striving for moral excellence, transcendence, and harmonious integration of wisdom from various cultural and philosophical sources.

In concluding this chapter, I'll address potential criticisms, acknowledging the necessity of personal context and contending with biases. Born and raised as an atheist, and since languishing in frustration as an agnostic naturalist, my journey into the *Hávamál* and its unexpected connection to Christian virtues challenges my preconceptions. The diverse examination of works from different cultures aims to mitigate biases, inviting readers to consider underlying generative principles that transcend cultural and religious divides.

As we grapple with the revelation that the wisdom of the *Hávamál* may lead back to Christianity, we find ourselves standing at a crossroads of belief. The exploration ahead promises to unravel more layers of this philosophical and spiritual tapestry, beckoning us to delve deeper into the interconnected truths that bridge the seemingly disparate realms of ancient wisdom and Christian theology. Repeating our methodology, let's examine *The Book of Five Rings* by Miyamoto Musashi next.

If will to truth is will to power, and power is acquired by sacrificing oneself to one's future self or a higher power (whether an Übermensch or God), then will to power is will to sacrifice, which is also the truth. Thus, the first angel goes and pours out his bowl on the earth.

CHAPTER FIVE

Second Revelation: The Samurai

We raise our second shield—*The Book of Five Rings*—fortifying our phalanx of reason and faith. Thus, the second angel blows his trumpet.

The Book Of Five Rings

The Book of Five Rings, authored by the legendary samurai Miyamoto Musashi, is a timeless martial arts classic that transcends its historical origins. Born in the early 17th century, Musashi is not merely a historical figure but a legendary swordsman and philosopher whose life has become intertwined with the essence of Japanese martial arts. Musashi's legacy is rooted in his unparalleled skill as a swordsman, his undefeated record in over sixty duels, and his remarkable insights into the art of war. The historical context in which Musashi lived was one of profound social and political change in Japan, marked by the decline of the samurai class and the rise of a new era. Within this dynamic period, Musashi's teachings emerged, leaving an indelible mark on the philosophy and practice of martial arts.

Musashi's reputation extends beyond his martial prowess to his mythical status as a *Kensei*—sword saint. The legendary tales of his duels and his iconic two-sword fighting style have elevated him to a near-mythical status in Japanese history.

However, Musashi's true legacy lies beyond his victories on the battlefield in his intellectual contributions to the understanding of strategy, combat, and life itself. In writing *The Book of Five Rings*, Musashi aimed not at personal power or conquest, as Nietzsche might suggest, but rather at the profound transmission of his insights into the truth of martial arts. The text is a testament to Musashi's commitment to preserving and sharing his knowledge, transcending his personal pursuits, and emphasizing the broader philosophical and strategic principles that underpin the martial path.

In the twilight of his life, Miyamoto Musashi devoted his attention to the contemplative and introspective task of penning *The Book of Five Rings*. His final years were characterized by a departure from the external battles that had defined much of his youth as he sought to distill a lifetime of martial wisdom into written words before his impending death. In the early 1640s, Musashi withdrew to the Reigando Cave in the remote mountains of Kyushu, Japan. Embracing a life of solitude, he delved into philosophy and strategy and the profound insights he had gained from years of rigorous training and numerous duels. It is said that Musashi wrote *The Book of Five Rings* as a testament to his comprehensive understanding of martial strategy, drawing not only from his experiences on the battlefield but also from the deep well of introspection that marked his later years. In this tranquil and reflective setting, conscious that his physical life might soon end, Musashi crafted a literary legacy that continues to influence martial artists, strategists, and philosophers today.

Contrary to Nietzschean notions of the will to power, Musashi's work reflects a dedication to martial arts' broader spiritual and philosophical dimensions. By recording his teachings, Musashi sought not dominion over others but the perpetuation of a legacy that could guide and inspire future generations of martial practitioners. In exploring *The Book of Five Rings*, we delve into Musashi's profound understanding of the martial Way, revealing a philosophy that extends far beyond the boundaries of personal power, echoing the timeless wisdom of a master swordsman whose legacy continues to resonate in both martial and philosophical spheres.

Cardinal Virtues

Justice or Chastity Versus Lust

- "Do not scheme for physical pleasure."
- "Have no heart for approaching the path of love."
- "Do not have preferences."

These three quotes exemplify the cardinal virtues of justice and chastity within the framework of moral guidance. The first quote advises against scheming for physical pleasure, urging individuals to refrain from unethical or manipulative means to satisfy personal desires. This aligns with justice and chastity by promoting fairness, honesty, and moral integrity. The second quote advises having no heart for approaching the path of love, representing something akin to lust in this context, encouraging individuals to exercise chastity and caution in romantic relationships. It underscores the virtue of chastity by advocating for purity and discretion in matters of the heart. The third quote broadens the scope by encouraging individuals to avoid forming preferences, promoting the virtue of justice by fostering impartiality and fair treatment of all. Collectively, these passages emphasize the cardinal virtues of justice and chastity by guiding individuals toward ethical behavior, moral integrity, and preserving purity in various aspects of life.

Fortitude or Abstinence Versus Gluttony

- "Do not have a liking for delicious food for yourself."
- "In all things concerning the body in martial arts, make the everyday body the body for martial arts, and the body for the martial arts the everyday body."
- "In the Way of Martial Arts, do not let your frame of mind be any different from your everyday mind."

These three quotes encapsulate the cardinal virtues of fortitude and abstinence within martial arts philosophy. The first quote discourages personal indulgence in delicious food, advocating a fortitudinous approach to resisting culinary temptations. It promotes abstinence, emphasizing self-discipline and overcoming desires for immediate gratification. The second quote extends this principle to integrating martial arts into daily life, emphasizing the importance of fortitude and self-control in maintaining a consistent and disciplined physical regimen. It encourages individuals to view their everyday body as the body for martial arts, promoting the virtue of abstinence from detrimental habits that may compromise physical well-being. The third quote further emphasizes the alignment of mental states between everyday life and martial arts, promoting a fortitudinous approach to maintaining a resilient and steadfast frame of mind. Together, these passages highlight the cardinal virtues of fortitude and abstinence within the context of martial arts philosophy.

Temperance or Liberality Versus Greed

- "Do not ever think in acquisitive terms."
- "Do not be intent on possessing valuables or a fief in old age."
- "Do not carry antiques handed down from generation to generation."

These three admonitions encapsulate the cardinal virtues of temperance and liberality by discouraging acquisitive and possessive tendencies. The first quote advises against thinking in acquisitive terms, emphasizing the importance of cultivating a mindset that transcends material accumulation. It aligns with the virtue of temperance, promoting a restrained and measured approach to acquiring possessions. The second warning extends this wisdom to old age, cautioning against an intense desire to possess valuables or a fief in later years. This advice underscores the virtue of temperance, encouraging individuals to detach themselves from material wealth and societal status. The third quote extends this guidance to family heirlooms, discouraging the carrying of antiques passed down through generations. This emphasizes the virtue of temperance by suggesting a detachment from the sentimental or material attachments that can hinder spiritual growth. These passages promote the cardinal virtues of temperance or liberality, advocating for a mindset free from excessive attachment to material possessions.

Prudence or Diligence Versus Sloth

- "Do not fast so that it affects you physically."
- "To learn about the principles of battle, meditate on this book; for the teacher is the needle, the student the thread. As a student, you should practice without end."
- "In the Way of victory through Martial Arts, you are intent on taking the initiative—always the initiative—in all things."

These three quotes exemplify the cardinal virtues of prudence and diligence by emphasizing a mindful and strategic approach to various aspects of life, particularly martial arts and self-discipline. The first quote advises against excessive fasting that could harm one's physical well-being, emphasizing a prudent and balanced approach to ascetic practices. It encourages individuals to be attentive to the needs of their bodies, aligning with the spiritual virtue of prudence that calls for thoughtful consideration of one's actions. The second quote underscores the diligence required to pursue knowledge of battle tactics. The analogy of the teacher as a needle and the student as the thread highlights the symbiotic relationship in learning, emphasizing continuous practice and dedication. Finally, the third quote reflects the importance of initiative in the Way of victory through martial arts, urging practitioners to be proactive in all aspects of life. This aligns with the cardinal virtue of diligence, promoting an active and focused mindset in pursuing success and mastery. These passages illuminate prudence or diligence by advocating for balanced practices, continuous learning, and proactive engagement in life's endeavors.

Spiritual Virtues

Charity or Patience Versus Wrath

- "If someone is skilled in this Way, he does not appear to be fast."
- "Here, too, a skillful person may appear slow, but he is never off beat. No matter what a well-trained person does, he never appears hurried."
- "If you do not know others, it is difficult to understand yourself."

These three quotes illuminate the spiritual virtues of charity, patience, and the avoidance of wrath. The first quote suggests that true skill in martial arts is not characterized by speed alone, emphasizing that a practitioner may not appear fast but possesses a deeper proficiency. This aligns with the virtue of patience, advocating for a calm and deliberate approach rather than hasty reactions. The second quote reinforces the importance of a well-trained person maintaining composure, regardless of the situation, promoting the virtues of patience and charity by discouraging hurried or aggressive behavior. The third quote introduces the concept that understanding oneself is intricately connected to knowing others, emphasizing the virtue of charity by encouraging practitioners to cultivate empathy and awareness of others' perspectives. These passages convey the spiritual virtues of patience, charity, and the avoidance of wrath, guiding martial artists toward a balanced and composed approach to their practice and interactions.

Hope or Kindness Versus Envy

- "Do not envy another's good or evil."
- "Do not complain or feel bitterly about yourself or others."
- "In the martial arts of one-on-one as well, you should think in terms of Becoming Your Opponent."

These three quotes resonate with the spiritual virtues of hope, kindness, and the rejection of envy within the context of martial arts philosophy. The first quote advises practitioners against harboring envy toward others' successes or misfortunes, promoting the virtues of hope and contentment. The quote encourages a mindset of appreciating one's journey without resentment by discouraging comparisons that can breed negativity. The second quote extends this philosophy by warning against complaints and bitterness, fostering kindness towards oneself and others. This aligns with self-compassion and understanding, creating a positive and constructive environment. The third quote emphasizes the importance of seeing one's opponent not as an adversary but as an opportunity for personal growth. This reflects the virtues of hope and kindness, encouraging practitioners to approach challenges with a mindset of continuous improvement and mutual respect. Together, these passages embody the spiritual virtues of hope, kindness, and the rejection of envy, guiding martial artists toward a positive and growth-oriented perspective in their practice and interactions.

Faith or Humility Versus Pride

- "Consider yourself lightly; consider the world deeply."
- "In my style, there is neither entrance nor depth to the sword, and there is no ultimate stance. There is only seeing through to its virtues with the mind."
- "In this world, there are no extraordinary ways of cutting someone down."

These three quotes encapsulate the spiritual virtues of faith and humility within the context of martial arts philosophy. The first quote advises individuals to consider themselves lightly and the world deeply, emphasizing a humble perspective and a recognition of the vastness of existence. This aligns with the virtue of humility, encouraging practitioners to approach life with a modest and open-minded mindset. The second quote delves into martial arts philosophy, emphasizing the absence of fixed techniques or ultimate stances. Instead, it advocates for perceiving the virtues of the sword with the mind, highlighting faith in the fluidity of learning and the importance of mental awareness. The third quote reinforces the spiritual virtues by asserting that there are no extraordinary ways of cutting someone down, promoting humility, and acknowledging that true mastery lies in simplicity rather than ostentation. Together, these passages guide individuals toward a spiritual approach characterized by faith in the learning process, humility in self-perception, and a recognition of the inherent simplicity in true mastery.

Christ-Like Virtues

Love, Gratitude, or Forgiveness

- "Do not turn your back on the various Ways of this world."
- "Do not regret things about your own personal life."
- "Do not lament parting on any road whatsoever."

These three quotes resonate with Christ-like virtues, particularly forgiveness, love, and gratitude, within the framework of martial arts philosophy. The first quote advises against turning away from the diverse experiences and paths in the world, promoting an open-hearted and accepting attitude reminiscent of Christ's teachings on embracing all aspects of life. The second quote encourages individuals not to dwell on regrets about personal life, aligning with the Christ-like virtue of forgiveness by promoting self-compassion and release from past mistakes. The third quote advises against lamenting partings on any road, emphasizing the Christ-like virtues of love and gratitude by encouraging a mindset focused on appreciating and cherishing the moments and connections experienced along life's journey. Together, these passages reflect Christ-like virtues, guiding martial artists to cultivate a spirit of forgiveness, love, and gratitude in their engagement with the diverse paths of life.

Transcendental Sacrifice

- "While on the Way, do not begrudge death."
- "Though you give up your life, do not give up your honor."
- "Never depart from the Way of the Martial Arts."
- "Two Heavens, One Style."
- "With the one, know the ten thousand—this is the principle of the martial arts, and an aspect of my own style I set down in this chapter."
- "With Yin-Yang, you step right and left, right and left, whether striking, pulling back or parrying a blow. I repeat: you should never step with just one foot."
- "In emptiness exists Good but no Evil. Wisdom is Existence. Principle is Existence. The Way is Existence. The Mind is Emptiness."

The Christ-like virtue of transcendental sacrifice intricately weaves itself into the fabric of the provided quotes from *The Book of Five Rings* by Miyamoto Musashi. The directive to "not begrudge death" while on the Way invokes the spirit of Jesus Christ. By sacrificing the fear of death, one rises above the boundaries between life and death, aligning with transcending our conscious-unconscious syzygy. It implies a surrender to the inevitability of mortality in pursuit of a higher cause or self-realization, mirroring the Holy Trinity in his Way of martial arts —"Two Heavens, One Style."

"Two Heavens, One Style" suggests a unity of dualities, reflecting the transcendence of opposites and the harmonization of conflicting elements. This echoes the concept of sacrificing individual distinctions for a more holistic understanding and mastery, resonating with the Christ-like virtue of sacrificing more extraordinary passions when virtues stand in opposition.

The quote, "Though you give up your life, do not give up your honor," underscores the sacrificial act of giving up one's life but insists on retaining honor. This aligns with the idea of sacrificing oneself for a higher cause, preserving a sense of virtue even in the face of the ultimate sacrifice. Integrating martial arts principles with the directive to "never depart from the Way of the Martial Arts" further emphasizes sacrificing life's ordinary, mundane aspects for the disciplined pursuit of a higher, martial ideal. In summary, these quotes collectively convey the essence of transcendental sacrifice, depicting a conscious-unconscious syzygy transcended in the face of death or adversity and the willingness to sacrifice for a higher cause or self-realization, drawing parallels with Christ-like virtues.

In the broader framework of Nietzschean philosophy, these seven quotes from *The Book of Five Rings* reveal thematic resonances with transcending syzygy and achieving a higher, unified state. The admonition in the first quote suggests a profound acceptance of mortality, aligning with the notion of sacrificing the fear of death to transcend the duality between life and death. Similarly, the second quote's emphasis on maintaining honor even when sacrificing one's life echoes the Nietzschean concept of creating values beyond good and evil, implying a sacrifice of life for a higher, honorable cause.

The directive to "never depart from the Way of the Martial Arts" implies a commitment to a disciplined path, akin to the dedication to creating values in the image of the Übermensch, involving the sacrifice of the mundane to pursue a higher, martial ideal. The statement "Two Heavens, One Style" suggests a unity of dualities, reflecting the transcendence of opposites and resonating with both Nietzsche's call to overcome traditional moralities and the notion of transcending through faith in a Holy Trinity. The principle of "knowing the ten thousand with the one" underscores a holistic understanding and mastery, aligning with transcending individual distinctions, resonant with Jesus's sacrifice and its ability to provide deeper meaning in various contexts.

The reference to Yin-Yang emphasizes balance and interconnectedness, echoing the idea of transcending dualities and finding harmony in syzygy, central to both Eastern philosophy and Nietzschean thought. Finally, the assertion that "in emptiness exists Good but no Evil" suggests that in transcending dualities, one finds a state where good exists without the contrast of evil. The emphasis on emptiness aligns with the idea of transcending conventional notions, resonating with Nietzsche's call to overcome traditional values. In summary, these quotes collectively reflect themes of transcendental syzygy, embracing sacrifice for higher ideals, and achieving a unified state, contributing to the contradiction between Nietzsche's Übermensch and the death of God, enriched by Taoist concepts of balance and unity.

This chapter presents a nuanced perspective on the concept of the Übermensch, drawing inspiration from Miyamoto Musashi's *The Book of Five Rings*. In this less literal version of the Übermensch, the prime motive appears to be the transcendence of dualities and attaining a higher, unified state. The Übermensch, as depicted in Musashi's philosophy, sacrifices the fear of death, embraces discipline in the martial arts, and strives for a holistic understanding of existence. The emphasis on "Two Heavens, One Style" suggests a unity of opposites, reflecting a desire to harmonize conflicting elements and rise above conventional distinctions. The Übermensch's morality, rooted in transcendental sacrifice, involves sacrificing ordinary, mundane aspects of life for the disciplined pursuit of a higher martial ideal. Honor is maintained even in the face of the ultimate sacrifice, and the commitment to the Way of the Martial Arts implies a dedication to a disciplined path, resonant with Nietzsche's call to create values beyond traditional moralities. The Übermensch, in this context, embodies a philosophy that transcends dualities, embraces sacrifice for higher ideals, and seeks a unified state, drawing inspiration from both Eastern and Western philosophical traditions.

If will to truth is will to power, and power is acquired by sacrificing oneself to one's future self or a higher power (whether an Übermensch or God), then will to power is will to sacrifice, which is also the truth. Thus, the second angel goes and pours out his bowl on the earth. Next, we'll repeat this process, analyzing *The Art of War* by Sun Tzu.

CHAPTER SIX

Third Revelation: The General

We raise our third shield—*The Art of War*—fortifying our phalanx of reason and faith. Thus, the third angel blows his trumpet.

The Art Of War

Sun Tzu's *The Art of War* is a cornerstone of strategic philosophy and timeless military wisdom, providing insights into the intricacies of warfare and the art of successful leadership. Dating back to ancient China, *The Art of War* transcends its historical context, offering a profound understanding of strategy, tactics, and the psychology of conflict. As we delve into this influential text, it becomes evident that its motivations and underlying principles may not align neatly with Nietzsche's concept of the will to power. Sun Tzu, often regarded as a military sage, did not pen his treatise with a personal thirst for dominance or individual glory, challenging the application of Nietzschean philosophy to his work.

The motivations behind *The Art of War* are deeply rooted in the collective well-being and strategic excellence of a ruler and his state. Sun Tzu's focus on strategic advantage and preserving life points towards a broader, more altruistic orientation than Nietzsche's individualistic will to power. To unravel the intricacies of this divergence, we will analyze key quotes from *The Art of War*, categorizing them within the framework of cardinal virtues, spiritual virtues, and Christ-like virtues. By juxtaposing Sun Tzu's timeless wisdom with Nietzsche's philosophy, we aim to illuminate the complexities of motivation, leadership, and the pursuit of excellence in war and personal development.

Cardinal Virtues

Justice or Chastity Versus Lust

- Sun Tzu says he can forecast victory or defeat by asking seven questions. Here is one: "Which of two sovereigns is imbued with the moral law?"
- "If the words of command are not clear and distinct, if orders *are* not thoroughly understood, the general is to blame. But if his orders are clear, and the soldiers nevertheless disobey, then it is the fault of their officers."
- "*The Moral Law* causes the people to be in complete accord with their ruler, so that they will follow him regardless of their lives, undismayed by any danger."

These three quotes from Sun Tzu's *The Art of War* emphasize the cardinal virtues of justice and chastity, particularly in the context of effective leadership and military strategy. The first quote delves into the moral character of sovereigns, highlighting the importance of moral law in leadership. Sun Tzu suggests that victory or defeat can be forecasted by assessing which sovereign is imbued with the moral law, underscoring the significance of just and virtuous leadership in achieving victory. The second quote addresses the clarity of communication and the responsibility of the general to ensure that orders are explicit and thoroughly understood. This echoes the cardinal virtue of justice, emphasizing fairness, clarity, and accountability in the chain of command. Lastly, the third quote underscores the alignment between the ruler and the people through the Moral Law, emphasizing a harmonious relationship that transcends individual lives and withstands danger. According to Sun Tzu's philosophy, these quotes epitomize the cardinal virtue of justice as an integral component of effective leadership and successful military strategy.

Fortitude or Abstinence Versus Gluttony

- "To muster his host and bring it into danger—this may be termed the business of the general."
- "Hence a wise general makes a point of foraging on the enemy."
- "Prohibit seeking for omens, and do away with superstitious doubts. Then, until death comes, no apparently predestined calamity need be feared."

These quotes shed light on the cardinal virtues of fortitude and abstinence, particularly in military strategy. The first quote underscores a general's need to muster his forces and lead them into challenging situations, emphasizing the virtue of fortitude—the courage to face and overcome danger. The second quote extends this idea, suggesting a wise general forages on the enemy, highlighting strategic aggression and resilience and the notion that abstinence prevents one from overburdening oneself. This also aligns with the cardinal virtue of fortitude, emphasizing endurance and strength in adverse situations. The third quote advocates for the prohibition of seeking omens and dispelling superstitious doubts, promoting a rational and resolute mindset. This reflects the virtue of both fortitude and abstinence, as it discourages indulgence in irrational fears or superstitious beliefs, suggesting that by doing so, one might acquire courage in the face of fear capable of transcending our greatest fear—death. In essence, these quotes portray the cardinal virtues of fortitude and abstinence as crucial elements in the successful conduct of military affairs, according to Sun Tzu's principles.

Temperance or Liberality Versus Greed

- "There are not more than five musical notes, yet the combinations of these five give rise to more melodies than probably can ever be heard. There are not more than three primary colors, yet in combinations they produce more hues than can ever be seen. There are not more than five tastes, yet combinations of them yield more flavors than can ever be tasted."

- "In battle, there are not more than two methods of attack —the direct and indirect, yet these two in combination give rise to an endless series of maneuvers."

- Sun Tzu says he can forecast victory or defeat by asking seven questions. Here is one: "In which army is there the greater constancy both in reward and punishment?"

Sun Tzu's insights in these quotes offer a perspective on the cardinal virtues of temperance and liberality versus greed. The first quote draws analogies from various domains, emphasizing the significance of simplicity and moderation. This aligns with the virtue of temperance, advocating for the restraint of excess and the appreciation of sufficiency. By highlighting the beauty and effectiveness that arise from limited music, color, and taste elements, Sun Tzu encourages a mindset of moderation and balance, discouraging greed for unnecessary complexity. The second quote, discussing methods of attack in battle, reinforces the virtue of temperance by acknowledging the effectiveness of simplicity and the focused application of strategies. Sun Tzu's question about constancy in reward and punishment speaks to the virtue of liberality versus greed. A leader who maintains constancy in these aspects demonstrates fairness and generosity, promoting loyalty and discouraging greed for disproportionate rewards. Overall, these quotes illustrate how Sun Tzu's principles encompass the cardinal virtues of temperance and liberality while cautioning against the pitfalls of greed.

Prudence or Diligence Versus Sloth

- "The art of war is of vital importance to the state. It is a matter of life and death, a road to either safety or to ruin. Hence it is a subject of inquiry which can on no account be neglected."
- Sun Tzu says he can forecast victory or defeat by asking seven questions. Here is one: "On which side is discipline most rigorously enforced."
- "The general who wins a battle makes many calculations in his temple ere the battle is fought. The general who loses a battle makes but few calculations beforehand."

These quotes underscore the cardinal virtues of prudence and diligence versus sloth. The first quote emphasizes the vital importance of the art of war to the state, portraying it as a matter of life and death with consequences leading either to safety or ruin. Sun Tzu positions the study of war as an inquiry that cannot be neglected, highlighting the virtue of diligence in understanding and preparing for potential challenges. The final set of quotes pertains to the calculations made before battle, linking closely to the virtue of prudence. Sun Tzu suggests that winning or losing a battle is contingent on the depth and rigor of the general's calculations and preparations. This accentuates the importance of discipline, thorough planning, and strategic foresight, promoting the virtues of prudence and diligence while cautioning against the dangers of sloth or lack of preparation. Sun Tzu's teachings advocate a proactive and disciplined approach, aligning with prudence and diligence in achieving success.

Spiritual Virtues

Charity or Patience Versus Wrath

- "There is no instance of a country having been benefited from prolonged warfare."
- "Hence to fight and conquer in all your battles is not

supreme excellence; supreme excellence consists in breaking the enemy's resistance without fighting."

- "He will win who knows when to fight and when not to fight."

These quotes convey the spiritual virtues of charity and patience versus wrath. The first quote suggests that prolonged warfare does not benefit a country, emphasizing the detrimental effects of ongoing conflict. Sun Tzu implies a higher virtue in seeking alternative paths to resolution, aligning with the spiritual virtue of patience and avoiding unnecessary wrath. The second quote advocates for supreme excellence, not in conquering through battles but in breaking the enemy's resistance without resorting to direct conflict. This aligns with the virtue of charity, promoting a mindset that seeks resolution and understanding rather than inflicting harm, offering an enemy people a lifeline without expectation of reciprocation. The third quote underscores the importance of discernment in warfare, knowing when to engage in battle and when to abstain. This wisdom reflects patience, strategic thinking, and an avoidance of wrathful impulsivity. Sun Tzu's teachings, therefore, resonate with the spiritual virtues of charity and patience, emphasizing the pursuit of peace and resolution over prolonged conflict and unnecessary aggression.

Hope or Kindness Versus Envy

- "Therefore soldiers must be treated in the first instance with humanity, but kept under control by iron discipline."
- "The captured soldiers should be kindly treated and kept. This is called, using the conquered foe to augment one's own strength."
- "Bestow rewards without regard for rule, issue orders without regard to previous arrangements and you will be able to handle a whole army."

These three quotes illustrate the spiritual virtues of hope and kindness versus envy. The first quote emphasizes the importance of treating soldiers with humanity, suggesting that a compassionate approach is foundational in leadership. This aligns with the virtue of kindness, promoting empathy and understanding even in the context of military discipline. The second quote further underscores the virtue of kindness by advocating for the humane treatment and retention of captured soldiers. Sun Tzu suggests using the conquered to strengthen one's forces, emphasizing the potential for positive transformation rather than harboring resentment or envy. The third quote encourages a leadership style characterized by generosity and flexibility, bestowing rewards and issuing orders without rigid adherence to established norms. This approach reflects hope and kindness, fostering a positive and harmonious environment instead of succumbing to envy or inflexible control. Therefore, Sun Tzu's teachings resonate with the spiritual virtues of hope and kindness, promoting a constructive and compassionate approach to warfare and leadership.

Faith or Humility Versus Pride

- "Hence the saying: If you know the enemy and know yourself, you need not fear the result of a hundred battles."
- "The natural formation of the country is the soldier's best ally, but a power of estimating the adversary, of controlling the forces of victory, and of shrewdly calculating difficulties, dangers, and distances, constitutes the test of a great general."
- "Hence the saying: If you know the enemy and you know yourself, your victory will not stand in doubt; if you know Heaven and know Earth, you may make your victory complete."

These three quotes embody the spiritual virtues of faith and humility versus pride. The first quote emphasizes the significance of self-awareness and understanding one's adversary, suggesting that battles' outcomes become less uncertain without this knowledge. This aligns with the virtues of faith and humility, encouraging trust in one's abilities and strategic insights without illusions of grandeur. The second quote underscores the importance of a general's capacity to assess and control various elements, demonstrating humility by acknowledging the challenges and uncertainties of warfare. The third quote expands this notion by incorporating an awareness of Heaven and Earth, reinforcing the virtue of humility by acknowledging the broader forces at play. Sun Tzu's teachings advocate for a humble and faithful approach, emphasizing the importance of self-awareness, understanding an enemy, and recognizing external factors for strategic success.

Christ-Like Virtues

Love, Gratitude, or Forgiveness

- "Regard your soldiers as your children, and they will follow you wherever you may lead. Look on them as your own beloved sons, and they will stand by you even unto death."
- "In the practical art of war, the best thing of all is to take the enemy's country whole and intact; to shatter and destroy it is not so profitable."
- "Spies are a most important element in war, because on them largely depends an army's ability to move."

These three quotes can be interpreted through the lens of Christ-like virtues, emphasizing love, gratitude, and forgiveness. The first quote encourages leaders to regard their soldiers as children and beloved sons, fostering a sense of love and familial connection within the military ranks. This perspective suggests that leadership founded on love and care can inspire loyalty and dedication. The second quote, advocating for preserving the enemy's country, reflects a Christ-like virtue of forgiveness. Instead of seeking destruction, Sun Tzu emphasizes the strategic advantage of maintaining the enemy's land intact, showcasing a merciful and forgiving approach. Finally, the third quote highlights the importance of spies in warfare, acknowledging their significance in obtaining crucial information. This recognition can be linked to the virtue of gratitude and forgiveness, as it appreciates the value of those who contribute to the success of a mission, even if they began the conflict helping the opposition. When viewed through this lens, Sun Tzu's teachings align with Christ-like virtues, promoting love, forgiveness, and gratitude in the context of strategic thinking and leadership.

Transcendental Sacrifice

- "All warfare is based on deception."
- "It is only one who is thoroughly acquainted with the evils of war who can thoroughly understand the profitable way of carrying it on."
- "The good fighters of old first put themselves beyond the possibility of defeat and then waited for an opportunity of defeating an enemy."
- "Hence his victories bring him neither reputation for wisdom nor credit for courage. He wins battles by making no mistakes. Avoidance of mistakes establishes the certainty of victory, for it means conquering an enemy that is already defeated."
- "Do not repeat the tactics which have gained you one victory, but let your methods be regulated by the infinite variety of circumstances."
- "Therefore, just as water retains no constant shape, so in warfare there are no constant conditions."
- "There are roads which must not be followed, armies which must not be attacked, towns which must not be besieged, positions which must not be contested, commands of the sovereign which must not be obeyed."

Summarizing Sun Tzu's entire philosophy, the first quote, "All warfare is based on deception," encapsulates a profound understanding of the Christ-like virtue of transcendental sacrifice, particularly the opposite implication that *all peace is based on truth.* By asserting that deception is foundational to warfare, Sun Tzu implies a sacrifice of immediate transparency for the sake of a higher truth—strategically pursuing peace. This aligns with the notion that sacrificing immediate, visible truth can lead to a more profound and lasting truth—the cessation of conflict and the establishment of peace.

The second quote, emphasizing the need to be thoroughly acquainted with the evils of war to understand its profitable conduct, reveals a sacrificial commitment to knowledge and wisdom. Sun Tzu suggests that one must sacrifice the comfort of ignorance and face the harsh realities of war to achieve a deeper understanding. The desire for a greater truth drives this sacrificial pursuit of knowledge—learning the art of war to minimize its negative impact and foster a more strategic and beneficial approach.

The third quote, advocating putting oneself beyond the possibility of defeat before seeking victory, illustrates a form of self-sacrifice for the greater good. By prioritizing personal preparedness and resilience, Sun Tzu suggests a willingness to sacrifice individual pleasure, happiness, or safety for the collective success of the mission, committing oneself to the endless and painstaking process of individual and collective betterment. This echoes the Christ-like virtue of transcendental sacrifice, where personal well-being is willingly offered for a higher purpose—the triumph of the entire army and the achievement of a lasting victory.

The fourth quote, focusing on winning through avoiding mistakes, highlights the sacrifice of personal reputation for the certainty of victory. Sun Tzu underscores that accomplishments achieved without errors may not bring recognition for wisdom or courage but contribute to the inevitability of success. This reflects the sacrifice of seeking personal acclaim or recognition in favor of a higher truth—achieving strategic victories through a flawless and mistake-free approach.

The fifth quote encourages adaptability in methods, reflecting a sacrifice of rigid adherence to past successes to respond to evolving circumstances. This embodies the Christ-like virtue of transcendental sacrifice by sacrificing the comfort of familiarity and routine for the greater good of strategic flexibility. Sun Tzu implies that sacrificing the security of familiar tactics can lead to a more profound truth—the ability to adapt and succeed in diverse situations.

The sixth quote, comparing water's ever-changing nature to warfare, signifies a willingness to sacrifice stability for flexibility and strategic advantage. Sun Tzu's analogy suggests that, like water, successful military strategies should be adaptable and dynamic. This reflects the sacrifice of a fixed and stable approach for the higher truth of achieving strategic advantage through fluidity and flexibility on the battlefield.

Finally, the seventh quote outlines restrictions in warfare, demonstrating a sacrifice of personal desires or ambitions for the greater good and adherence to ethical considerations. Sun Tzu implies that certain actions must be avoided, showcasing a sacrifice of potentially advantageous but unethical choices to maintain moral integrity. This aligns with the Christ-like virtue of transcendental sacrifice, where personal ambitions are sacrificed for a higher truth—ethical conduct and the pursuit of a just and honorable victory. When viewed through transcendental sacrifice, each quote reveals strategic principles prioritizing higher ideals and long-term goals over immediate gains or personal interests, aligning with the Christ-like virtues emphasized in this analysis.

The chapter combines Sun Tzu's *The Art of War* with an analysis that juxtaposes its principles with Nietzsche's concept of the Übermensch. The Übermensch, as conceived by Nietzsche, is an individual who transcends conventional morality and societal norms, driven by the will to power and the pursuit of individual excellence. In the context of Sun Tzu's teachings, the analysis suggests that the motivations behind *The Art of War* may not neatly align with Nietzsche's concept. Sun Tzu's focus on collective well-being, strategic excellence, justice, and virtues like temperance, prudence, and kindness implies a more altruistic orientation than Nietzsche's individualistic will to power. As inferred from the analysis, the prime motive of this knightly-aristocratic version of the Übermensch might be centered around strategic excellence and the collective well-being of the ruler and the state, emphasizing justice, temperance, and kindness. The morality associated with this Übermensch would involve adherence to fairness, clarity, discipline, and a compassionate approach to leadership and warfare, diverging from Nietzsche's more individualistic and potentially amoral perspective.

Nevertheless, transcendental sacrifice plays a crucial role in the aim or teleology of this version of the Übermensch, as depicted through the lens of Sun Tzu's teachings. Sun Tzu's philosophy highlights strategic principles that prioritize higher ideals and long-term goals over immediate gains or personal interests. The concept of transcendental sacrifice is evident in Sun Tzu's emphasis on self-awareness, the pursuit of knowledge about the evils of war, and the willingness to put oneself beyond the possibility of defeat. Sacrificing personal comfort, reputation, and stability for the greater good of strategic success and ethical conduct aligns with the Übermensch's transcendence of conventional values. Sun Tzu's advocacy for a flexible and adaptable approach and avoiding mistakes reflects a sacrifice of immediate desires or habits for the higher truth of achieving lasting victories. In this context, transcendental sacrifice becomes a guiding principle in the Übermensch's pursuit of excellence, emphasizing a strategic mindset prioritizing enduring success and ethical considerations over short-term gains or personal glory.

If will to truth is will to power, and power is acquired by sacrificing oneself to one's future self or a higher power (whether an Übermensch or God), then will to power is will to sacrifice, which is also the truth. Thus, the third angel goes and pours out his bowl on the earth. Next, we'll repeat this process and analyze *The Analects* of Confucius.

CHAPTER SEVEN

Fourth Revelation: The Gentleman

W e raise our fourth shield—*The Analects* of Confucius —fortifying our phalanx of reason and faith. Thus, the fourth angel blows his trumpet.

The Analects

In exploring the construction of Nietzsche's Übermensch through the prism of *The Analects*, we delve into two distinct philosophical traditions, each offering its unique insights into the ideals of human perfection. *The Analects*, a collection of teachings and ideas attributed to Confucius, are foundational texts in Confucianism, outlining moral conduct, optimized social relationships, and personal virtues. His work is situated within the historical context of ancient China, where Confucius sought to address the socio-political upheavals of his time by imparting wisdom that transcended individual lives and resonated with enduring moral principles.

Confucius's conception of "the sage" in *The Analects* parallels Nietzsche's Übermensch, portraying an idealized figure whose character embodies the highest virtues and moral principles. Much like the Übermensch, the sage represents an unattainable vision of human perfection that serves as a guiding ideal for individuals to strive toward. Both philosophical traditions recognize the transformative power of these ideals, urging individuals to transcend their current limitations and strive for moral and intellectual excellence.

The will to power, a central concept in Nietzsche's philosophy, encounters a distinct perspective in *The Analects*. Confucius's motivation in compiling these teachings cannot be solely explained by a desire for power in the Nietzschean sense. Instead, Confucius aimed to foster a harmonious and morally upright society by emphasizing the cultivation of virtue in individuals. This departure from Nietzsche's focus on power dynamics sets the stage for a nuanced exploration of how *The Analects* may inform the construction of the Übermensch, integrating Confucian values with Nietzschean concepts.

Our analysis will proceed by dissecting key quotes from *The Analects*, reorganizing them as cardinal, spiritual, and Christ-like virtues. This comparative examination will illuminate the intersections and divergences between Nietzsche's Übermensch and Confucius's sage, shedding light on the philosophical richness that emerges when these two traditions intersect. Through this exploration, we aim to unravel the complexities of constructing the Übermensch within the moral and ethical landscape presented by *The Analects*.

Cardinal Virtues

Justice or Chastity Versus Lust

- "The gentleman is conscious of [not breaking] the law, while the common man is conscious of what benefits he might reap [from the state]."
- "The gentleman understands what is morally right. The petty man understands what is profitable."
- "A person should stay close to those who do their best and are trustworthy. He should not befriend those who are not his equals. And when he makes a mistake, he should not be

afraid to correct it."

In these excerpts from *The Analects*, Confucius imparts wisdom that aligns with the cardinal virtues of justice and chastity, emphasizing the moral conduct of the gentleman. The first quote underscores the gentleman's awareness of upholding the law and moral principles, highlighting a commitment to justice over personal gain. This contrasts with the common man, who may be more concerned with reaping benefits from the state. The second quote deepens the exploration of justice by emphasizing the gentleman's understanding of what is morally right, prioritizing ethical considerations above mere profitability. Confucius, advising individuals toward virtuous conduct, promotes a sense of justice that transcends pragmatic concerns.

While not explicitly addressing chastity, the third quote speaks to choosing associates wisely, reflecting an aspect of justice. Confucius advises staying close to those who demonstrate trustworthiness and excellence, implying that the gentleman should uphold standards of justice in both personal conduct and in the selection of companions. The notion of not befriending those who are not equals suggests a commitment to justice in relationships, seeking associations that align with one's moral values. These quotes from *The Analects* illustrate Confucius's emphasis on justice and moral discernment, providing insights into the cardinal virtues that contribute to constructing a virtuous and just Übermensch sage.

Fortitude or Abstinence Versus Gluttony

- "A gentleman does not try to stuff himself when he eats and is not worried about the comfort of his dwelling."
- "To spend the whole day stuffing yourself and not to put your mind to use at all—this is hopeless behavior."
- Confucious's disciples said about him, "He did not overeat if the rice was polished or if the meat was finely cut. He did not eat rice that had gone off, nor fish or meat that had

spoiled. He did not eat food with a sickly color or a foul odor, nor anything that was overcooked or undercooked. He did not eat food that was not in season, nor did he eat except at meal times. He did not eat meat that was not properly cut off or meat paired with the wrong sauce. Even when there was plenty of meat, he would not eat more meat than grain. Only in the case of wine was there no limit laid down, but he never drank to the point of being addled. He would not touch wine that had been sitting overnight nor dried meat bought from a shop. And even when he kept a plate of ginger on the table [after the meal was over], he did not eat too much of it."

These excerpts illustrate Confucius's teachings on the cardinal virtues of fortitude and abstinence, emphasizing moderation in various aspects of life. The first quote focuses on the gentleman's attitude toward eating and dwelling. By discouraging the act of overindulging and expressing indifference to personal comfort, Confucius promotes abstinence and fortitude. The second quote further emphasizes the futility of indulging in excessive eating without engaging one's mind in productive pursuits, reinforcing the importance of fortitude in resisting self-destructive behaviors. The disciples' account of Confucius's dietary habits provides a concrete example of abstinence and moderation. Confucius's meticulous approach to food selection, avoidance of overeating, and adherence to proper culinary practices demonstrate his commitment to maintaining balance and avoiding gluttony. The emphasis on not consuming spoiled or improperly prepared food aligns with the virtue of abstinence, emphasizing the importance of self-discipline and discernment in matters of sustenance. Overall, these passages offer insights into how Confucius envisioned the cultivation of fortitude and abstinence as integral components of virtuous living.

Temperance or Liberality Versus Greed

- "A person who is not humane cannot remain for long either in hard or in easy circumstances. A humane person feels at home in humanness. A wise person [practices it because he] sees benefits in humanness."
- "If the gentleman forsakes humanness, how can he be worthy of the name gentleman? The gentleman does not abandon humanness, not even for the duration of a meal. He holds onto it whether he is in a hurry or in a crisis."
- "Only in the deepest winter do we realize that the pine and cypress are the last to shed their leaves."

These quotes highlight Confucius's teachings on the cardinal virtues of temperance and liberality, emphasizing the importance of humane conduct and the rejection of greed. The first quote underscores the connection between humanity and enduring well in both difficult and comfortable circumstances. Confucius posits that a person lacking in humane qualities cannot sustain themselves over the long term, promoting the virtue of temperance—the ability to exercise self-restraint and moderation in all circumstances. The notion that a humane person feels at home in humanness further emphasizes the value of consistently practicing virtues.

The second quote reinforces the virtue of temperance by emphasizing the unyielding commitment of a true gentleman to humane conduct. Confucius argues that even in challenging situations or during meals, the gentleman does not abandon humanness, illustrating the importance of maintaining virtue under all circumstances. This commitment aligns with the cardinal virtue of temperance, as it requires the restraint of one's desires and adherence to ethical principles even in times of urgency or crisis.

The third quote, using the metaphor of the pine and cypress retaining their leaves in the deepest winter, conveys the virtue of temperance. The analogy suggests that, like these trees, individuals should hold onto their virtues, including generosity and kindness, especially during challenging times. By connecting the endurance of leaves to the virtue of temperance, Confucius encourages a consistent and unwavering commitment to virtuous conduct, reinforcing the idea that true virtue stands firm even in adverse conditions.

Prudence or Diligence Versus Sloth

- "To make a mistake and not to correct it—now that is called making a mistake."
- "A person who does not think ahead about the distant future is sure to be troubled by worries close at hand."
- "He first puts his words into action. He then lets his words follow his action."

These quotes emphasize Confucius's teachings on the cardinal virtues of prudence and diligence, contrasting them with the pitfalls of sloth or lack of foresight. The first quote succinctly captures the essence of prudence by highlighting the importance of recognizing and correcting mistakes. Confucius suggests that failing to rectify errors is a significant mistake, promoting the virtue of prudence as the key to self-improvement and avoiding repeated errors.

The second quote underscores diligence by encouraging forward thinking and considering the distant future. Confucius implies that a person who neglects to plan for the long term will likely encounter troubles and difficulties in the present. This perspective aligns with the virtue of diligence, emphasizing the importance of careful and persistent effort in anticipating and addressing future challenges.

The third quote reinforces the virtues of prudence and diligence by advocating for aligning words with actions. Confucius emphasizes the significance of translating one's intentions into concrete deeds, promoting the idea that genuine virtue involves more than mere verbal expressions. This aligns with the cardinal virtues of prudence, the wisdom to discern the right course of action, and diligence, the persistent effort to actualize virtuous conduct.

Spiritual Virtues

Charity or Patience Versus Wrath

- "If you do not correct yourself, how can you hope to correct others?"
- "If you guide the people with ordinances and statutes and keep them in line with [threats of] punishment, they will try to stay out of trouble but will have no sense of shame. If you guide them with exemplary virtue and keep them in line with the practice of the rites, they will have a sense of shame and will know to reform themselves."
- "Have unshakeable trust in [the moral path you pursue]. Love learning. Hold on to the way of good until you die. Do not enter a state of threatened danger. Do not reside in a state embroiled in conflict. Show yourself when the moral way is evident. Seek reclusion when it is not. When the moral way prevails in a state, being poor and lowly is a cause for shame. When the moral way does not prevail in the world, having wealth and position is a cause for shame."

These quotes illuminate Confucius's teachings on the spiritual virtues of charity, patience, and the avoidance of wrath. The first quote encourages introspection and self-correction as a prerequisite for guiding and correcting others. Confucius emphasizes the importance of personal growth and moral development, fostering the virtue of patience in dealing with both one's own shortcomings and those of others.

The second quote underscores the spiritual virtues of charity and patience by promoting the idea that moral guidance should be rooted in exemplary virtue and the practice of rites. Confucius contrasts this approach with the use of ordinances, statutes, and threats of punishment, suggesting that genuine moral transformation arises from a deep sense of shame rather than mere compliance. This aligns with the virtues of charity, guiding others with benevolence and virtue when one could choose instead to become a tyrant. It also aligns with patience, advocating for a gradual and transformative approach to moral education.

The third quote further explores patience and avoidance of wrath by emphasizing the importance of trust in one's moral path, love for learning, and adherence to goodness throughout life. Confucius advises seeking reclusion in times of moral decline and showcasing moral virtue when it prevails. This reflects the virtue of patience, urging individuals to patiently await the opportune moments to manifest and promote moral excellence. Additionally, it suggests a charitable attitude towards moral principles, advocating for a sense of shame when wealth and position are gained in a morally decadent society.

Hope or Kindness Versus Envy

- "Virtue does not stand alone. It is bound to have neighbors."
- "Is humaneness far away? As soon as I desire humaneness, it is here."
- "People are similar by nature; they become distinct through practice."

These three quotes emphasize Confucius's teachings on the spiritual virtues of hope, kindness, and the avoidance of envy. In the first quote, Confucius implies that virtue is not isolated but interconnected with other positive qualities. This reflects hope, suggesting that cultivating virtuous qualities can lead to the development of others, creating a network of positive attributes.

The second quote epitomizes the virtue of hope. Confucius suggests that the pursuit of humaneness is readily achievable by the simple act of desiring it. This expression instills hope in the accessibility of virtuous qualities, encouraging individuals to aspire to goodness and kindness in their actions and interactions.

The third quote underscores hope further by emphasizing the malleability of human nature. Confucius implies that individuals can distinguish themselves positively through dedicated practice, aligning with this virtue. Arguably one of Confucius's most hopeful expressions, it indicates that by adopting sage-like qualities, there is hope of differentiating oneself positively and contributing to a virtuous society.

Faith or Humility Versus Pride

- "To say that you know something when you know it and to say that you do not know something when you do not know it—this is true knowing."
- "I dare not call myself a sage or a humane man. What could be said of me is that I work toward it without ever feeling sated, and I am never tired of teaching."
- "To fail to cultivate virtue, to fail to practice what I have learned, not to direct my steps toward what is right when I know what that is, and to make mistakes and not be able to correct them—these are the things that worry me."

These three quotes highlight the spiritual virtues of faith and humility while cautioning against pride. In the first quote, Confucius emphasizes the importance of humility in knowledge. He suggests that true understanding comes from acknowledging one's limits and avoiding the pride that might accompany claims of knowledge beyond one's grasp. The second quote reflects the virtue of humility. Despite his apparent wisdom, Confucius refrains from the self-proclaimed titles of sage or humane man. Instead, he humbly acknowledges his continuous journey toward virtue and the ongoing commitment to self-improvement. The third quote further highlights the importance of humility and faith in pursuing virtue. Confucius expresses concern about falling short of virtuous ideals and humbly acknowledges the continuous effort required for self-improvement.

Christ-Like Virtues

Love, Gratitude, or Forgiveness

- "Do not impose on others what you yourself do not want [others to impose on you]."
- About humaneness, the Master said, "Love others." About wisdom, the Master said, "Know others."
- "If you truly set your mind on being humane, you are not morally culpable."

These three quotes encapsulate Christ-like virtues of love, gratitude, and forgiveness. The first quote echoes the Christian principle of treating others as you wish to be treated —the Golden Rule. As expressed by Jesus in his Sermon on the Mount, the Golden Rule is encapsulated in the words, "So whatever you wish that men would do to you, do so to them; for this is the law and the prophets" (Matthew 7:12, RSV). This fundamental ethical principle encourages individuals to treat others with the same kindness, fairness, and compassion they desire for themselves, emphasizing empathy and reciprocity in human interactions. It reflects the virtue of love by emphasizing empathy and considering others' feelings and desires.

The second quote underlines the interconnectedness of love and wisdom. Christ emphasized love for others, and Confucius similarly positioned humaneness and wisdom as intertwined virtues. Understanding and knowing others is a path to fostering love and compassion, aligning with Christ's teachings. The third quote speaks to the virtue of forgiveness. By encouraging a genuine commitment to humaneness, Confucius suggests that such a mindset alleviates moral culpability, emphasizing the transformative power of love and forgiveness in moral conduct.

Transcendental Sacrifice

- "If I do not take part in the sacrifice, it is as if I did not sacrifice at all."

- "A man of high purpose and a man with deep humaneness would not seek to stay alive at the expense of humaneness. There are times when they would sacrifice their lives to have humaneness fulfilled."

- "The humane man takes on the difficult task first and will not attend to any benefits [until he has completed his task]."

- "This is no longer a matter of humaneness. You must be referring to a sage. Even Yao and Shun found it difficult to accomplish what you've just described. A humane person wishes to steady himself, and so he helps others steady themselves. Because he wishes to reach his goal, he helps others to reach theirs. The ability to make an analogy from what is close at hand is the method and the way of realizing humaneness."

- "Set your aim for the Way, hold on to your integrity, rely on your humaneness, and get your share of play in the arts."

- "Learn as if you will never catch up, as though you are afraid of losing whatever you have already understood."

- "If you hold on to doing your best and being trustworthy [in words] as your principle and try always to direct your intent and action to what is right, you will be taking virtue to a higher level. When you like a person, you want him to live. When you dislike a person, you want him to die. To wish him to live at one moment and to wish him to die at the next, this is clouded judgment."

The concept of sacrifice is deeply woven into the fabric of Confucian virtue, as expressed in the idea that active participation in sacrifice is essential for its meaningful realization. By asserting, "If I do not take part in the sacrifice, it is as if I did not sacrifice at all," Confucius underscores the importance of personal involvement and commitment in ethical and ritual acts, aligning with our definition of transcendental sacrifice in that it requires a sacrifice of the self.

The sacrificial spirit is further emphasized by Confucius

when he extols the virtues of individuals who, driven by high purpose and deep humaneness, are willing to sacrifice their own lives for the greater fulfillment of humaneness. In stating, "A man of high purpose and a man with deep humaneness would not seek to stay alive at the expense of humaneness," he elevates the significance of self-sacrifice for society's ethical and moral advancement.

Confucius highlights the humane person's prioritization of challenging tasks over personal benefits, reinforcing the principle that true sacrifice involves putting the welfare of others before one's own. "The humane man takes on the difficult task first and will not attend to any benefits [until he has completed his task]" encapsulates the idea that sacrifice involves a deliberate choice to address collective needs (or another higher cause) before individual gain.

A sage's profound sacrifice becomes apparent when Confucius challenges the listener's reference to humaneness by stating, "This is no longer a matter of humaneness. You must be referring to a sage." This suggests that the sage's pursuit of higher ideals involves sacrifices beyond conventional notions of humaneness, symbolizing the transcendental nature of their commitment to virtue.

The integration of sacrifice into the pursuit of virtue is further illustrated by Confucius when he urges individuals to align their aspirations with the Way, maintain integrity, rely on humaneness, and find joy in the arts. This reflects a holistic approach to sacrifice, encompassing life and personal development from various angles. Confucius further emphasizes the perpetual nature of learning and self-improvement, suggesting that learning through sacrifice should be relentless and continuous. "Learn as if you will never catch up, as though you are afraid of losing whatever you have already understood" reinforces the idea that sacrificing one's time and effort for learning is a virtuous endeavor contributing to personal and societal advancement.

The complexity of human emotions and judgments in

the context of sacrifice is acknowledged by Confucius when he critiques inconsistent attitudes toward others. "If you hold on to doing your best and being trustworthy [in words] as your principle and try always to direct your intent and action to what is right, you will be taking virtue to a higher level," suggests that sacrificing personal biases and judgments is integral to the virtuous path, emphasizing the need for consistent, compassionate, and selfless behavior.

In this knightly-aristocratic version of the Übermensch constructed through the fusion of Nietzschean philosophy and Confucian teachings, the aim (teleology) is to cultivate an individual characterized by a harmonious blend of Christ-like, cardinal, spiritual, and transcendental virtues. The Übermensch, inspired by both Nietzsche's will to power and Confucius's emphasis on moral conduct, seeks to transcend conventional values and achieve a higher state of being. The prime motive of this Übermensch involves the relentless pursuit of virtue, wisdom, and excellence, with a commitment to the well-being of others and the betterment of society. In the context of this Übermensch, morality is intricately woven with virtues such as love, kindness, justice, fortitude, patience, and humility. Transcendental sacrifice plays a central and transformative role in his teleology, as evidenced by the emphasis on active participation in rituals, the willingness to sacrifice personal well-being for collective good, and the integration of sacrifice into various aspects of life. The Übermensch's morality revolves around a selfless commitment to higher ideals, continuous learning, and consistent, compassionate treatment of others, reflecting a profound synthesis of Nietzschean and Confucian principles.

In summary, these quotes from Confucius reflect the Christ-like virtues of transcendental sacrifice by emphasizing the active participation in rituals, the willingness to sacrifice personal well-being for the greater good, the prioritization of collective needs, the pursuit of higher ideals beyond conventional virtues, the holistic integration of sacrifice into various aspects of life, the continuous commitment to learning and self-improvement, and the consistent, compassionate treatment of others.

If will to truth is will to power, and power is acquired by sacrificing oneself to one's future self or a higher power (whether an Übermensch or God), then will to power is will to sacrifice, which is also the truth. Thus, the fourth angel goes and pours out his bowl on the earth. Next, we'll repeat the process and analyze *The Prince* by Niccolò Machiavelli.

CHAPTER EIGHT

Fifth Revelation: The Prince

We raise our fifth shield—*The Prince*—fortifying our phalanx of reason and faith. Thus, the fifth angel blows his trumpet.

The Prince

The Prince, by Niccolò Machiavelli, is arguably one of history's most misunderstood philosophical texts, dedicated initially to Lorenzo de' Medici, an Italian statesman, banker, de facto ruler of the Florentine Republic, and the foremost patron of Renaissance culture in Italy, who wielded significant influence and power during that era. By constructing an idealized version of a prince, he urged Lorenzo the Magnificent and future readers to transcend the duality of good and evil, bringing us to the boundary between them so that we might conquer both fortune and our enemies by knowing the other side. Controversy still exists as to whether or not he crossed this boundary. Yet, the wisdom in his words nevertheless rings true.

"I fear that my writings about it [the methods and rules for a prince] may be deemed presumptuous, differing as I do, especially in this matter, from the opinions of others. But my intention being to write something of use to those who understand it, it appears to me more proper to go to the real truth of the matter than its imagination."

The influence of Christianity on *The Prince,* within the context of the Italian Renaissance, further illuminates the tension between traditional moral values and Machiavelli's pragmatic, often controversial, approach to governance. The Church held considerable sway during the Italian Renaissance, and Christian ethics permeated political discourse. However, Machiavelli's work is notable for departing from the prevailing Christian moral framework. While Christian virtues emphasize otherwise, Machiavelli's prince operates in a world where political survival often demands actions that challenge these traditional virtues.

Machiavelli's embrace of a Nietzschean admiration for warriors marks a departure from conventional Christian ethics. By offering a leadership vision that prioritizes the ruler's strength and cunning, his philosophy provides an ideal framework for constructing our Übermensch prince. Although controversial in its departure from Christian ideals, Machiavelli's nuanced perspective presents a balanced bias, as it reflects the shifting intellectual landscape of the Renaissance, where the fusion of classical thought and emerging secular philosophies began to challenge the dominance of religious doctrine. In constructing an Übermensch according to the Machiavellian perspective, our prince embodies a transcendence of traditional morality, striving for power and effectiveness in the intricate dance of political maneuvering.

Still, one thing remains clear beyond debate: a prince should always aim toward the virtues of God, but when these virtues are at odds between the individuals and society, he should adopt *meta-virtues* for the betterment of society by sacrificing his own. In this sense, Machiavelli's prince is almost Christ-like, taking on the world's sins to deliver his people into God's grace. What could be more righteous than sacrificing one's personal salvation, confronting the evil that lurks in the shadows with equal measure so that one's people might be saved?

Cardinal Virtues

Justice or Chastity Versus Lust

- "I believe this arises from the cruelties being used well or badly. Well used may be called those (if it is permissible to use the word well of evil) which are committed once for the need of securing one's own self, and which afterwards are not persisted in, but are exchanged for measures as useful to the subjects as possible. Cruelties ill-used are those which, although at first few, increase rather than diminish with time. Those who follow the former condition may remedy in some measure their condition, both with God and man; as did Agathocles. As to the others, it is impossible for them to maintain themselves."

- "The chief foundations of all states, whether new, old, or mixed, are good laws and good arms. And as there cannot be good laws where there are not good arms, and where there are good arms there should be good laws, I will not discuss the laws, but will speak of the arms."

- "For every time that one has the judgment to know the good and evil that anyone does or says, even if he has no intention, yet he recognizes the bad and good works of his minister and corrects the one and supports the other; and the minister cannot hope to deceive him and therefore remains good."

These quotes from Machiavelli's *The Prince* delve into the cardinal virtues of justice and chastity versus lust as viewed through the lens of political governance. In the first quote, Machiavelli distinguishes between two forms of cruelty: those that are well-used and those that are ill-used. The former, cruelty committed for self-preservation and not persistently continued, aligns with a just ruler who employs cruelty sparingly for the greater good. However, the latter form, cruelty ill-used, represents an unjust ruler whose oppressive actions increase over time, leading to instability and an inability to maintain power. Machiavelli underscores the importance of justice in governance, advocating for rulers who use cruelty judiciously and in service of their subjects.

The second quote reinforces the cardinal virtue of justice by emphasizing the foundational elements of a state: good laws and good arms. Here, Machiavelli asserts that effective governance requires both legal justice and military strength. A just ruler must implement laws that benefit the state and its subjects while maintaining a strong military to ensure security and stability. The correlation between good laws and good arms reflects the cardinal virtue of justice as an essential component of successful statecraft.

The third quote speaks to the virtue of justice in the context of a ruler's judgment and discernment. Machiavelli suggests that a just ruler possesses the judgment to distinguish between good and evil actions, even when performed unintentionally. This ability allows the ruler to correct the wrongs and support the righteous acts of their ministers, fostering an environment where deception is impossible. The emphasis on the ruler's discernment aligns with the cardinal virtue of justice, highlighting the importance of fair judgment and correcting wrongdoing within the political realm.

Fortitude or Abstinence Versus Gluttony

- "A prince being thus obliged to know well how to act as a beast must imitate the fox and the lion, for the lion cannot protect himself from snares, and the fox cannot defend himself from wolves. One must therefore be a fox to recognize snares, and a lion to frighten wolves."
- "You must know, then, that there are two methods of fighting, the one by law, and the other by force: the first method is that of men, the second of beasts; but as the first method is often insufficient, one must have recourse with the second."

- "A man who wishes to make a profession of goodness in everything must necessarily come to grief among so many who are not good. Therefore, it is necessary for a prince, who wishes to maintain himself, to learn how not to be good, and to use it and not use it according to the necessity of the case."

In these quotes, the cardinal virtues of fortitude and abstinence versus gluttony are explored within the context of political leadership. The first quote likens a prince to both a fox and a lion, highlighting the necessity for strategic adaptability. The fox represents cunning and the ability to recognize snares. At the same time, the lion symbolizes strength and the capacity to intimidate adversaries. This combination of qualities suggests that a ruler must exhibit courage in the face of challenges while also practicing abstinence from rash actions, akin to the virtues of fortitude and abstinence.

The second quote delves into the cardinal virtue of fortitude by introducing the two fighting methods: by law and by force. Machiavelli asserts that while the legal method is human, the forceful method is akin to the behavior of beasts. The prince must be capable of both approaches, demonstrating fortitude when confronted with challenges that demand bold actions. Applying these methods showcases fortitude and the strength to navigate political complexities using various strategies.

The third quote introduces the notion that a prince, to maintain power, must sometimes abandon an overt commitment to goodness. Machiavelli argues that in a world where not everyone is virtuous, a prince needs to be pragmatic and, if necessary, act against conventional moral standards. This perspective aligns with the cardinal virtue of abstinence, emphasizing the ability to refrain from strictly adhering to moral ideals when the political situation demands a more pragmatic approach. It underscores the necessity for leaders to exercise restraint and adaptability to navigate the complexities of governance effectively.

Temperance or Liberality Versus Greed

- Speaking of mercenaries and auxiliaries, he says, "A wise prince, therefore, always avoids these forces and has recourse of his own, and would prefer rather to lose with his own men than conquer with the forces of others, not deeming it a true victory, which is gained by foreign arms."
- "There is nothing which destroys itself so much as liberality, for by using it you lose the power of using it, and become either poor and despicable, or, to escape poverty, rapacious and hated."
- "But above all he must abstain from taking the property of others, for men forget more easily the death of their father than the loss of their patrimony."

In these quotes from *The Prince*, Machiavelli's political insights provide perspectives on the cardinal virtues of temperance and liberality versus greed. In the first quote, Machiavelli advises against relying heavily on foreign forces such as mercenaries and auxiliaries. According to him, a wise prince practices temperance by avoiding overdependence on external resources, preferring his own forces even if victory may be uncertain. This emphasizes the virtue of temperance—moderation and self-control—when pursuing power.

The second quote delves into the potential pitfalls of liberality, cautioning that excessive generosity can lead to the erosion of one's power. Machiavelli suggests that liberality, when not exercised with temperance, can result in the loss of resources and influence. This aligns with the cardinal virtue of temperance, emphasizing the importance of moderation in using resources and generosity to maintain a ruler's strength and reputation. In this way, he makes a case for adopting meta-virtues aligned with one's future self or a higher cause when virtues stand at odds.

The third quote touches upon the cardinal virtue of liberality and its limits, as Machiavelli advises against seizing the property of others. The prince, he argues, should exercise temperance by refraining from actions that might provoke resentment or jeopardize the stability of his rule. This underscores the notion that true leadership involves a balance between generosity and restraint, and a wise prince must navigate these virtues judiciously to ensure both power and stability.

Prudence or Diligence Versus Sloth

- "One ought never to allow a disorder to take place in order to avoid war, for war is not thereby avoided, but only deferred to your disadvantage."
- "It is not unknown to me how many have been and are of the opinion that worldly events are so governed by fortune and by God, that men cannot by their prudence change them, and that on the contrary there is no remedy whatever, and for this they may judge it to be useless to toil much about them, but let things be ruled by chance." He later explains, "It happens similarly with fortune, which shows her power where no measures have been taken to resist her, and turns her fury where she knows that no dams or barriers have been made to hold her."
- "This is found in the nature of things, that one never tries to avoid one difficulty without running into another, but prudence consists in being able to know the nature of the difficulties, and taking the least harmful as good."

Machiavelli reflects on the cardinal virtues of prudence and diligence versus sloth, emphasizing the importance of proactive and strategic thinking in politics. The first quote cautions against allowing disorder to fester, avoiding war in the process, highlighting the need for prudence and the understanding that deferring action can lead to greater disadvantages. Machiavelli urges leaders to act diligently and decisively to address challenges promptly.

The second quote challenges the fatalistic view that

events are solely governed by fortune or God, advocating for an active and prudent approach to shaping outcomes. Machiavelli rejects the idea that circumstances are beyond human influence, emphasizing the virtue of diligence in resisting the capricious nature of fortune. He stresses that leaders should take measures to control and guide events rather than resigning themselves to passivity.

The third quote delves into the interconnected nature of difficulties and the role of prudence in choosing the least harmful path. Machiavelli suggests that prudence lies in understanding the complexities of challenges and selecting courses of action that minimize harm. This reinforces the virtue of prudence and diligence in navigating the intricacies of political affairs, encouraging leaders to be proactive and strategic in their decision-making.

Spiritual Virtues

Charity or Patience Versus Wrath

- "For injuries should be done all together, so that being less tasted, they will give less offense. Benefits should be granted little by little, so that they may be better enjoyed. And above all, a prince must live with his subjects in such a way that no accident should make him change it, for good or evil; for necessity arising in adverse times, you are not in time of severity, and the good that you do does not profit you, as it is judged to be forced, and you will derive no benefit whatever from it."
- "It is the nature of men to be as much bound by the benefits they confer as those they receive."
- "For it must be noted, that men must either be caressed or else annihilated; they will revenge themselves for small injuries, but cannot do so for great ones; the injury therefore that we do to a man must be such that we need not fear his vengeance."

Machiavelli provides insights into the spiritual virtues of charity and patience versus wrath. The first quote suggests a strategic approach to both inflicting injuries and bestowing benefits. Machiavelli advises that injuries should be delivered collectively to minimize their impact, displaying a certain patience and calculation in the application of harm. Conversely, benefits should be granted gradually to enhance their appreciation, reflecting a charitable approach to governance.

The second quote delves into benevolence's reciprocal nature, emphasizing charity's spiritual virtue. Machiavelli observes that individuals are bound by the benefits they confer as much as those they receive, fostering a sense of gratitude and reciprocity. This aligns with the concept of charity, as the prince is encouraged to engage in acts of kindness and generosity to cultivate a positive relationship with his subjects.

The third quote explores the delicate balance between kindness and severity, suggesting that men must either be treated with kindness or, if necessary, annihilated. This advice reflects the virtue of patience. Machiavelli proposes a measured and calculated response to potential threats, avoiding impulsive and wrathful actions. By advocating for strategic benevolence and patient governance, Machiavelli touches upon the spiritual virtues of charity and patience in the context of effective leadership.

Hope or Kindness Versus Envy

- "From which another notable rule can be drawn, that princes should let the carrying out of unpopular duties devolve on others, and bestow favors themselves."
- "Thus it is well to seem pious, faithful, humane, religious, sincere, and also to be so; but you must have the mind so watchful that when it is needful to be otherwise you may be able to change to the opposite qualities."
- "A prince must take great care that nothing goes out of his mouth, which is not full of the above-named five qualities,

and, to see and hear him, he should seem to be all faith, all integrity, all humanity, and all, religion. And nothing is more necessary than to seem to have this last quality, for men in general judge more by the eyes than by the hands, for everyone can see, but very few have to feel."

In these quotes, Machiavelli explores the spiritual virtues of hope and kindness versus envy within the context of political leadership. The first quote suggests a strategy for princes to maintain a positive image by delegating unpopular duties to others while personally bestowing favors. This approach aligns with the virtue of kindness, as it involves the prince demonstrating benevolence and generosity, fostering hope among the people.

The second quote delves into the complexity of appearances and the need for a prince to balance genuine virtues with the ability to adapt when necessary. Machiavelli advises rulers to appear pious, faithful, humane, and sincere while being vigilant and ready to adopt opposite qualities if the situation demands. This advice touches on the virtue of hope, as the prince is encouraged to present an optimistic and virtuous facade to inspire confidence and trust among the populace.

The third quote emphasizes the importance of perception, stating that a prince must carefully control his words and outward demeanor to project qualities such as faith, integrity, humanity, and religion. This aligns with the virtue of kindness, as the prince is advised to create an image of benevolence and virtuous conduct. Overall, Machiavelli's insights into political strategy and cultivating a positive image touch upon the spiritual virtues of hope and kindness, providing a nuanced perspective on effective leadership.

Faith or Humility Versus Pride

- "Therefore a wise prince will seek means by which his subjects will always and in every possible condition of things have need of this government, and then they will always be faithful to him."

- "If men were all good, this precept would not be a good one; but as they are bad, and would not observe their faith with you, so you are not bound to keep faith with them. Nor are legitimate grounds ever wanting to a prince to give colour to the non-fulfillment of his promise."

- "A new prince has never been known to disarm his subjects, on the contrary, when he has found them disarmed he has always armed them, for by arming them these arms become faithful and those that were faithful remain so, and from being merely subjects become your partisans."

In these excerpts, Machiavelli delves into the spiritual virtues of faith and humility versus pride. The first quote suggests that a wise prince should ensure that his subjects always depend on the government, fostering a sense of reliance that strengthens their fidelity. This aligns with the virtue of humility, too, as the prince is advised to maintain a position of importance in the lives of his subjects without succumbing to pride.

The second quote introduces a Machiavellian perspective on the nature of faith, asserting that a prince is not obligated to keep faith with those who would not reciprocate in a world where people are inherently flawed. This challenges the traditional virtue of faith, emphasizing the pragmatic consideration of self-interest and the state over blind trust. In this way, he draws an essential distinction between blind faith and real faith. Yet again, he reinforces that faith should be reciprocated as a good.

The third quote highlights a new prince's strategic use of arms, suggesting that disarmed subjects should be armed to create loyalty. In this manner, he urges new princes to lead with faith in the people, offering their subjects heightened independence in exchange for their trust. This also aligns with the virtue of humility, as the prince is encouraged to recognize and respond to the needs and vulnerabilities of the subjects rather than succumbing to prideful notions of invincibility, hoarding the means of self-defense to himself. Overall, Machiavelli's insights into political leadership provide a complex and sometimes controversial perspective on the spiritual virtues of faith and humility.

Christ-Like Virtues

Love, Gratitude, or Forgiveness

- "I will say, in conclusion, that it is necessary for a prince to possess the friendship of the people; otherwise he has no resource in times of adversity."
- "Therefore, the best fortress is to be found in the love of the people, for although you may have fortresses they will not save you if you are hated by the people."
- "Because there is no other way of guarding one's self against flattery than by letting men understand that they will not offend you by speaking the truth; but when everyone can tell you the truth, you lose their respect." Later, he clarifies, "A prince, therefore, ought always to take counsel, but only when he wishes, not when others wish; on the contrary he ought to discourage absolutely attempts to advise him unless he asks it, but he ought to be a greater asker, and a patient hearer of the truth about those things which he has inquired of; indeed, if he finds that anyone has scruples in telling him the truth he should be angry."

In these excerpts, Machiavelli touches upon Christ-like virtues such as love, gratitude, and forgiveness within the context of political leadership. The first quote underscores the necessity for a prince to cultivate the friendship of the people, emphasizing the importance of their affection as a resource during challenging times. This aligns with the virtue of love, suggesting that a leader's strength lies in the genuine goodwill of the populace.

The second quote strengthens the association between

love and political strength, asserting that the love of the people serves as the best fortress. This implies that a leader's power is most secure when grounded in the positive sentiments of those they govern. Machiavelli thus acknowledges the value of reciprocal love in securing a leader's position.

The third quote introduces the theme of truth-telling, suggesting that a leader should create an environment where people feel free to speak the truth. This aligns with the virtue of forgiveness, as a leader should not hold grudges against those who offer honest advice, even if it is critical. By encouraging openness and forgiveness, a leader can foster trust and cooperation. Overall, Machiavelli's insights on love, gratitude, and forgiveness in leadership reflect a pragmatic application of these virtues in the art of governance.

Transcendental Sacrifice

- "I fear that my writings about it [the methods and rules for a prince] may be deemed presumptuous, differing as I do, especially in this matter, from the opinions of others. But my intention being to write something of use to those who understand it, it appears to me more proper to go to the real truth of the matter than its imagination."
- "For the Romans did in these cases what all wise princes should do, who consider not only present but also future discords and diligently guard against them; for being foreseen they can easily be remedied, but if one waits till they are at hand, the medicine is no longer in time as the malady has become incurable; it happening with this as with those hectic fevers, as doctors say, which at their beginning are easy to cure but difficult to recognize, but in course of time when they have not at first been recognized and treated, become easy to recognize and difficult to cure. Thus it happens in matters of state; for knowing afar off (which it is only given to a prudent man to do) the evils that are brewing, they are easily cured. But when, for want of

such knowledge, they are allowed to grow so that every one can recognize them, there is no longer any remedy to be found. Therefore, the Romans, observing disorders while yet remote, were always able to find a remedy, and never allowed them to increase in order to avoid a war; for they knew that war is not to be avoided, and can be deferred only to the advantage of the other side; they therefore declared war against Philip and Antiochus in Greece, so as not to have to fight them in Italy, though they might at the time have avoided either; this they did not choose to do, never caring to do that which is now every day to be heard in the mouths of our wise men, namely to enjoy the advantages of delay, but preferring to trust their own virtue and prudence; for time brings with it all things, and may produce indifferently either good or evil."

- Speaking of the acquisition of ecclesiastical principalities, he says, "They are acquired either by ability or by fortune; but are maintained without either, for they are sustained by the ancient religious customs, which are so powerful and of such quality, that they keep their princes in power in whatever manner they proceed and live." Later, he says, "Only these principalities, therefore, are secure and happy. But as they are upheld by higher causes, which the human mind cannot attain to, I will abstain from speaking of them; for being exalted and maintained by God, it would be the work of a presumptuous and foolish man to discuss them."

- "A Prince should therefore have no other aim or thought, nor take up any other thing for his study, but war and its order and discipline, for that is the only art that is necessary to one who commands, and it is such a virtue that it not only maintains those who are born princes, but often enables men of private fortune to attain that rank."

- "And yet he must not mind incurring the disgrace of those vices, without which it would be difficult to save the state, for if one considers well, it will be found that some things which seem virtues would, if followed, lead to one's ruin, and some others which appear vices result, if followed, in one's greater security and well being."

- "A prince, therefore, must not mind incurring the charge of cruelty for the purpose of keeping his subjects united and confident; for, with a very few examples, he will be more merciful than those who, from excess of tenderness, allow disorders to arise, from whence spring murders and rapine; for these as a rule injure the whole community, while the executions carried out by the prince injure only one individual."

- "Whence it may be seen that hatred is gained as much by good works as by evil, and therefore, as I said before, a prince who wishes to maintain the state is often forced to do evil, for when the party, whether populace, soldiery, or nobles, whichever it be that you consider necessary to you for keeping your position, is corrupt, you must follow its humour and satisfy it, and in that case good works will be inimical to you."

Now, let's interpret Machiavelli's quotes from *The Prince* through the lens of Christ-like virtues, specifically transcendental sacrifice. In expressing fear that his writings may be deemed presumptuous, Machiavelli reveals a profound willingness to transcend personal concerns to impart valuable knowledge. This aligns with Christ-like virtues, emphasizing the sacrifice of personal reputation to serve a higher purpose —the dissemination of wisdom. By acknowledging potential criticism, Machiavelli prioritizes truth over personal acclaim, reflecting a sacrificial commitment to genuine understanding. Thus, he does not provide these insights following a will to power, as Nietzsche would have us believe, but following a will to truth.

When discussing the Romans' approach to foreseeing future discords, Machiavelli advocates for a proactive sacrifice of immediate peace for long-term harmony. This reflects a Christ-like virtue of sacrificing the comfort of the present for the greater good of future stability. The Romans' foresight demonstrates a willingness to endure initial discomfort, embodying the concept of transcendent sacrifice by prioritizing collective well-being over short-term ease, a principle resonant with Christ's teachings.

Regarding ecclesiastical principalities, Machiavelli displays humility by recognizing the influence of higher, divine causes and abstaining from detailed discussion. This implicit sacrifice of comprehensibility for the acknowledgment of the limitations of human understanding resonates with Christ-like humility before the mysteries of the divine. By refraining from delving into matters beyond human grasp, Machiavelli willingly sacrifices the clarity of discourse to honor the reverence due to transcendent forces.

Machiavelli proposes a single-minded focus on the study of war for a prince, advocating the sacrifice of a well-rounded education to pursue skills crucial to effective governance. This aligns with Christ-like virtues by emphasizing the sacrifice of personal interests for the greater purpose of statecraft. The commitment to mastering the art of war, even at the expense of a broader education, exemplifies a sacrificial dedication to the higher cause of ensuring the security and stability of the state. Moreover, it places a heavy burden on the prince, requiring him from an early age to sacrifice even what may seem righteous to defend his people.

In addressing the acceptance of disgrace for the sake of unity, Machiavelli suggests that a prince should not fear incurring the charge of cruelty if necessary for maintaining unity among subjects. This highlights a Christ-like virtue of sacrificing personal likability for the pragmatic necessity of maintaining control. The willingness to bear the weight of a negative reputation underscores a commitment to the greater good—a stable and united state—where individual sacrifice serves the collective well-being. Did Jesus not take on the same role, bearing the weight of all humanity's sins for us?

Machiavelli acknowledges the necessity of evoking

hatred when required to maintain power, illustrating the sacrifice of personal reputation and moral standing for political survival. This pragmatic approach aligns with the notion of sacrificing individual morality for the stability and well-being of the state. This concept echoes the transcendental sacrifice observed in Christ's teachings. Machiavelli's acknowledgment of the political reality underscores the complex interplay between virtue and pragmatic governance.

Lastly, Machiavelli recognizes that good works can sometimes lead to hatred, emphasizing the sacrifice of virtuous deeds for a nobler purpose. This pragmatic perspective underscores the notion that certain virtues may need to be set aside for the greater good. In the complex world of political maneuvering, the sacrifice of personal righteousness for the stability and longevity of the state becomes a central tenet, echoing the Christ-like virtue of transcendent sacrifice for the betterment of society.

In conclusion, Niccolò Machiavelli's *The Prince* is a multifaceted exploration of political philosophy intertwined with profound insights into the complexities of leadership. Machiavelli's willingness to face potential criticism for disseminating valuable yet controversial knowledge aligns with a Christ-like virtue of transcendent sacrifice. In advocating for proactive sacrifice for long-term harmony, recognizing divine influences with humility, and prioritizing the study of war for the greater good, Machiavelli reflects a commitment to the higher purpose of statecraft, mirroring Christ's sacrifice for the salvation of humanity.

The emphasis on sacrificing personal likability, moral standing, and even virtuous deeds for the stability and longevity of the state underscores the pragmatic reality of governance through meta-virtues. It echoes the Christ-like virtue of transcendent sacrifice for societal well-being, challenging readers to grapple with the intricate balance between moral ideals and political pragmatism.

In this knightly-aristocratic version of the Übermensch,

drawing inspiration from Machiavelli's *The Prince*, the prime motive of the Übermensch prince is the pursuit of power and effectiveness in the intricate dance of political maneuvering. The Übermensch, shaped by Machiavellian philosophy, embodies a transcendence of traditional morality, with a morality that is defined by pragmatism, adaptability, and the relentless pursuit of statecraft. The Übermensch prince aims to navigate the complexities of political governance with strategic cunning, strength, and a Nietzschean admiration for warriors. While the prince is advised to aim towards the virtues of God, the context acknowledges that political survival often demands actions that challenge traditional virtues, emphasizing the Übermensch's ability to rise above conventional morality for the state's greater good using meta-virtues.

Nevertheless, transcendental sacrifice plays a central role in this teleology. The Übermensch prince is called upon to sacrifice personal reputation, immediate peace for long-term stability, and even virtues that might lead to hatred if they jeopardize the stability of the state. This sacrificial approach aligns to maintain power and ensure the state's well-being. The prince's morality is characterized by a calculated balance between virtuous appearances and pragmatic actions, where the ends justify the means. The Übermensch prince, embracing Machiavellian ideals, aims to transcend conventional moral boundaries, making calculated sacrifices to secure the survival and prosperity of the political entity they govern.

As we transition to the next chapter focusing on *Meditations* by Marcus Aurelius, Machiavelli's insights serve as a foundational shield fortifying our logical argument. The exploration of virtues and sacrifices in *The Prince* prepares us for a deeper dive into the wisdom of Marcus Aurelius, further enriching our phalanx of logos and virtue. Like Machiavelli, Nietzsche looked to ancient Rome as the pinnacle of the knightly-aristocratic mode of valuation. So we will follow his logic, aiming to destroy it once and for all, by again demonstrating how the knightly-aristocratic mode of valuation is more similar to the priestly mode of valuation than he believed. With the trumpet's sound, we step into the realm of Stoicism, ready to explore the philosophical treasures of another era.

Speaking of Marcus Aurelius, whom we will discuss in the next chapter, Machiavelli said, "From these causes it resulted that Marcus, Pertinax, and Alexander, being all modest of life, lovers of justice, enemies of cruelty, humane, and benign, had all a sad ending except Marcus. Marcus alone lived and died in honour, because he succeeded to the empire by hereditary right and did not owe it either to the soldiers or to the people; besides which, possessing many virtues, which made him revered, he kept both parties in their place as long as he lived and was never either hated or despised."

If will to truth is will to power, and power is acquired by sacrificing oneself to one's future self or a higher power (whether an Übermensch or God), then will to power is will to sacrifice, which is also the truth. Thus, the fifth angel goes and pours out his bowl on the earth.

CHAPTER NINE

Sixth Revelation: The Emperor

We raise our sixth shield—*Meditations*—fortifying our phalanx of reason and faith. Thus, the sixth angel blows his trumpet.

Meditations

Meditations, by Marcus Aurelius, stands as a profound collection of private reflections and philosophical insights from the Roman Emperor, written during his campaigns on the northern frontiers of the Roman Empire. Composed as a series of personal notes rather than a formal treatise, *Meditations* is a remarkable work that delves into Stoic philosophy, exploring themes of virtue, self-discipline, and the nature of existence. For historical context, *Meditations* was written in the late 2nd century AD, during a period marked by internal and external challenges to the Roman Empire. As the most powerful man in the world at the time, Marcus Aurelius faced the responsibility of leading the empire through these tumultuous times.

Marcus Aurelius did not seek external power through *Meditations* despite being an emperor. The work was a private journal never intended for publication. This intimate aspect of the text adds a layer of authenticity to the reflections, offering a glimpse into the inner thoughts of a ruler grappling with the complexities of governance and personal virtue. In contrast to Nietzsche's concept of the will to power, where the pursuit of power is seen as a driving force, Marcus Aurelius, in his position of immense authority, explores the inner realm of personal virtue and ethical conduct.

The non-Christian origins of *Meditations* are rooted in Stoicism. This philosophical school emerged in ancient Greece and later gained prominence in Rome. Stoicism emphasizes cultivating wisdom, courage, justice, and temperance as the path to virtuous living. Its teachings influenced many prominent figures in antiquity, including Marcus Aurelius. Despite these non-Christian philosophical roots, *Meditations* reflects a timeless exploration of ethical principles and the human condition.

Furthermore, when examining *Meditations* in the context of Nietzschean philosophy, one finds a compelling connection between Marcus Aurelius and Nietzsche's concept of the Übermensch. In his works, Nietzsche expounds on the idea of the Übermensch as an individual who transcends conventional morality, embraces their own values, and creates their own meaning in a world devoid of inherent meaning. As a personification of the knightly-aristocratic mode of valuation, Marcus Aurelius aligns closely with Nietzsche's vision of the Übermensch. While the Roman Emperor may not explicitly reject traditional morality, his focus on internal virtues and personal discipline reflects a parallel emphasis on self-overcoming and cultivating an individual's unique moral code. *Meditations*, with its emphasis on self-reflection and the pursuit of inner excellence, becomes a reservoir of wisdom from which one could construct the foundations of the Übermensch, drawing from the lived experiences and philosophical musings of a ruler navigating the complexities of power and virtue in the ancient world.

Our endeavor to construct a vision of the Übermensch using quotes from Marcus Aurelius aims to identify the virtues and insights found in his reflections. By examining the

Stoic virtues embedded in *Meditations*, we seek to challenge Nietzsche's proclamation that "God is dead." Instead, we aim to demonstrate that the ethical and moral principles articulated by Marcus Aurelius provide a foundation for a meaningful and purposeful existence. In doing so, we explore spirituality and ethics, asserting that the timeless wisdom found in *Meditations* can contribute to a contemporary understanding of human flourishing and the enduring relevance of moral principles.

Cardinal Virtues

Justice or Chastity Versus Lust

- "The directing and sovereign part of yourself must stay immune to any current in the flesh, either smooth or troubled, and keep its independence: it must define its own sphere and confine those affections to the parts they affect."
- "In the constitution of the rational being I can see no virtue that counters justice: but I do see the counter to pleasure—self-control."
- "Yes, death and life, fame and ignominy, pain and pleasure, wealth and poverty—all these come to good and bad alike, but they are not in themselves either right or wrong: neither then are they inherent good or evil."

These three quotes from Marcus Aurelius' *Meditations* illuminate the cardinal virtues of justice and chastity versus lust, as seen through the lens of Stoic philosophy. In the first quote, Aurelius emphasizes the importance of maintaining a sovereign and independent rational self, impervious to the tumultuous currents of the flesh. This reflects the virtue of chastity, as he encourages the discipline of one's desires and affections, resisting the influence of external temptations. The second quote delves into the virtue of justice by asserting that no virtue contradicts justice within the constitution of the rational being. Moreover, Aurelius identifies self-control as the counter to pleasure, reinforcing the Stoic principle of temperance. The third quote expands on the Stoic perspective, stating that external circumstances such as life, death, pleasure, or pain are indifferent and not inherently good or evil. This perspective aligns with the virtue of justice, emphasizing the Stoic commitment to an objective and rational evaluation of external events rather than succumbing to the lures of pleasure or lust. Together, these quotes articulate Marcus Aurelius' Stoic understanding of justice and chastity as cardinal virtues, guiding individuals to transcend the fleeting desires of the flesh for a higher, more principled existence.

Fortitude or Abstinence Versus Gluttony

- "Be like the rocky headland on which the waves constantly break. It stands firm, and round it the seething waters are laid to rest."
- "So in all future events which might induce sadness remember to call on this principle: 'this is no misfortune, but to bear it true to yourself is good fortune.'"
- "How good it is when you have roast meat or suchlike foods before you, to impress on your mind that this is the dead body of a fish, this is the dead body of a bird or pig; and again, that the Falernian wine is the mere juice of grapes, and your purple edged robe simply the hair of a sheep soaked in shell-fish blood!"

These three quotes exemplify the cardinal virtues of fortitude and abstinence versus gluttony. The first quote employs the metaphor of a rocky headland to illustrate the virtue of fortitude. It encourages individuals to stand firm amid the turbulent waves of life, embodying resilience and steadfastness. The second quote reinforces the virtue of fortitude by urging the remembrance that events inducing sadness are not misfortunes but opportunities to bear true to oneself, emphasizing the Stoic commitment to inner strength and endurance. The third quote extends the Stoic principle of abstinence by advising the contemplation of food and drink as mere biological components rather than indulging in gluttony. This practice aligns with the virtue of temperance, emphasizing self-discipline and control over desires. These quotes illuminate Marcus Aurelius' Stoic ideals of fortitude and abstinence as integral components of virtuous living, promoting resilience, endurance, and disciplined self-control while confronting life's challenges.

Temperance or Liberality Versus Greed

- "No wholly good person would regret missing a pleasure. Therefore pleasure is neither beneficial nor good."
- "Moreover, the pursuit of pleasure as a good and the avoidance of pain as an evil constitutes sin."
- "The second is resistance to the promptings of the flesh. It is the specific property of rational and intelligent activity to isolate itself and never be influenced by the activity of the senses or impulses: both of these are of the animal order, and it is the aim of intelligent activity to be sovereign over them and never yield them the mastery—and rightly so, as it is the very nature of intelligence to put all these things to its own use."

These three quotes provide insights into the cardinal virtues of temperance and liberality versus greed within the context of Stoic philosophy. The first quote challenges the conventional view of pleasure as a good, asserting that a wholly virtuous person would not regret missing a pleasure, thus questioning the intrinsic value of pleasure. This aligns with the virtue of temperance, emphasizing a measured and restrained approach to desires. The second quote further classifies the pursuit of pleasure and the avoidance of pain as sinful, emphasizing the Stoic notion that true virtue transcends the purpose of transient pleasures. The third quote underscores the virtue of temperance by highlighting the importance of resisting the promptings of the flesh and maintaining rational sovereignty over sensory and impulsive desires. Marcus Aurelius encourages cultivating an intelligent and disciplined approach to life, embodying the Stoic virtues of temperance and self-mastery over greed and excess.

Prudence or Diligence Versus Sloth

- "I do my own duty: the other things do not distract me. They are either inanimate or irrational, or have lost the road and are ignorant of the true way."
- "Constantly test your mental impressions—each one individually, if you can: investigate the cause, identify the emotion, apply the analysis of logic."
- "No more roundabout discussion of what makes a good man. Be one!"

In these three quotes from Marcus Aurelius, the cardinal virtues of prudence and diligence versus sloth are illuminated through Stoic principles. The first quote reflects an unwavering commitment to duty, showcasing diligence in focusing on one's responsibilities and not allowing distractions to sway from the path of virtue. This aligns with the virtue of diligence, emphasizing a steadfast dedication to one's obligations. The second quote emphasizes the importance of constant self-examination and logical analysis of mental impressions, promoting a diligent and prudent approach to understanding one's thoughts and emotions. The third quote serves as a direct call to action, urging the reader to embody virtue rather than engage in prolonged theoretical discussions—a practical manifestation of prudence through decisive and virtuous conduct. Marcus Aurelius encourages a proactive and diligent engagement with the principles of Stoicism, emphasizing the virtues of prudence and diligence over the pitfalls of sloth and inaction.

Spiritual Virtues

Charity or Patience Versus Wrath

- "Do not give up in disgust or impatience if you do not find action on the right principles consolidated into a habit in all that you do."
- "Whatever I do, either by myself or with another, should have this sole focus—the common benefit and harmony."
- "Every creature must do what follows from its own constitution. The rest of creation is constituted to serve rational beings (just as everything else the lower exists for the higher), but rational beings are here to serve each other. So the main principle in man's constitution is the social."

These three quotes encapsulate the spiritual virtues of charity and patience versus wrath. The first quote encourages perseverance and patience in cultivating virtuous habits, advising against impatience when progress seems slow. This aligns with the virtue of patience, urging individuals to remain steadfast in their commitment to virtuous action. The second quote emphasizes a selfless focus on the common benefit and harmony in all actions, reflecting the virtue of charity through a genuine concern for the well-being of others. Finally, the third quote underscores humanity's social nature, highlighting the interconnectedness of rational beings and the duty to serve one another. These principles advocate for patience in the face of challenges, a charitable orientation towards others, and a recognition of the inherent social responsibility within the human constitution, collectively embodying the spiritual virtues of charity and patience versus wrath.

Hope or Kindness Versus Envy

- "Kindness is invincible—if it is sincere, not fawning or pretense."
- "All that you pray to reach at some point in the circuit of your life can be yours now—if you are generous to yourself."
- "To put it shortly: all things of the body stream away like

a river, all things of the mind are dreams and delusion; life is warfare, and a visit in a strange land; the only lasting fame is oblivion. What then can escort us on our way? One thing, and one thing only: philosophy. This consists in keeping the divinity within us inviolate and free from harm, master of pleasure and pain, doing nothing without aim, truth, or integrity, and independent of others' action or failure to act. Further, accepting all that happens and is allotted to it [the divinity within us] as coming from that other source which is its own origin: and at all times awaiting death with the glad confidence that it is nothing more than the dissolution of the elements of which every living creature is composed. Now if there is nothing fearful for the elements themselves in their constant changing of each into another, why should one look anxiously in prospect at the change and dissolution of them all? This is in accordance with nature: and nothing harmful is in accordance with nature."

These three quotes encourage the spiritual virtues of hope and kindness versus envy. The first quote underscores the invincibility of sincere kindness, emphasizing this virtue's genuine and selfless nature. The second quote encourages a sense of contentment and kindness towards oneself, suggesting that generosity and self-compassion can help achieve what one aspires. Finally, the third quote delves into the philosophical perspective on life, advocating for a mindset grounded in hope and kindness. It posits that life's challenges are transient, and the enduring source of strength lies in philosophy—the pursuit of wisdom and virtue. The overarching theme is cultivating hope, extending kindness to oneself and others, and recognizing the transformative power of philosophical understanding in navigating life's complexities, collectively embodying these spiritual virtues.

Faith or Humility Versus Pride

- "The pride that prides itself on freedom from pride is the hardest of all to bear."
- "One should pay no attention to any of those things which do not belong to man's portion incumbent on him as a human being."
- "Vanity is the greatest seducer of reason: when you are most convinced that your work is important, that is when you are most under its spell."

These three quotes illuminate the spiritual virtues of faith and humility versus pride. The first quote exposes the paradoxical nature of pride, cautioning against the arrogance that arises from claiming freedom from pride itself. It suggests that true humility comes from recognizing and restraining one's pride rather than proclaiming superiority. The second quote emphasizes the importance of focusing on aspects within the human sphere, urging individuals to humbly disregard elements beyond their control and concentrate on fulfilling their fundamental human responsibilities. Lastly, the third quote delves into the seductive nature of vanity, warning against the hubris that clouds reason and distorts one's perception of the significance of their work. Together, these quotes articulate a philosophy of humility, encouraging individuals to embrace faith in their human capabilities while remaining vigilant against pride and vanity.

Christ-Like Virtues

Love, Gratitude, or Forgiveness

- "Say to yourself first thing in the morning: today I shall meet people who are meddling, ungrateful, aggressive, treacherous, malicious, unsocial. All this has afflicted them through their ignorance of true good and evil. But I have that the nature of good is what is right, and the nature of evil what is wrong; and I reflected that the nature of the offender himself is akin to my own—not a kinship of blood or seed, but a sharing in the same mind, the same fragment of divinity. Therefore I cannot be harmed by any of them, as none will infect me with their wrong. Nor can I be angry with my kinsman or hate him. We were born for cooperation, like feet, like hands, like eyelids, like the rows of upper and lower teeth. So to work in opposition to one another is against nature: and anger or rejection is opposition."

- "In this world there is only one thing of value, to live out your life in truth and justice, tolerant of those who are neither true nor just."
- "The best revenge is not to be like your enemy."

These three quotes encapsulate the Christ-like virtues of love, gratitude, and forgiveness. In its entirety, "Book I" of *Meditations* expresses profound gratitude that sets the stage for understanding these virtues. The first quote exemplifies forgiveness and empathy, guiding individuals to recognize the ignorance of those who may act negatively and to cultivate a sense of kinship with them rooted in the shared fragment of divinity within each person. The second quote emphasizes the value of living a life of truth and justice, urging tolerance towards those who may not embody these virtues. Finally, the third quote introduces the concept of non-revenge, echoing the Christian principle of turning the other cheek and promoting a path of love and understanding rather than retaliation. These quotes illuminate a Christ-like approach to interpersonal relationships, emphasizing love, gratitude, and forgiveness in the face of adversity.

Transcendental Sacrifice

- "Loss is nothing more than change."
- "Nothing should be done without purpose."
- "Most of what we say and do is unnecessary: remove the superfluity, and you will have more time and less bother."
- "Do not imagine that, if something is hard for you to

achieve, it is therefore impossible for any man: but rather consider anything that is humanly possible and appropriate to lie within your own reach too."

- "Disgraceful if, in this life where your body does not fail, your soul should fail first."
- "Your mind will take on the character of your most frequent thoughts: souls are dyed by thoughts."
- "He lives with the gods who consistently shows them his soul content with its lot, performing the wishes of that divinity, that fragment of himself which Zeus has given each person to guard and guide him. In each of us this divinity is our mind and reason."

In his *Meditations*, Marcus Aurelius presents a series of reflections that convey the essence of transcendental sacrifice —a concept aligned with Stoic philosophy and resonant with Christ-like virtues. The idea that "loss is nothing more than change" encapsulates a Stoic perspective, urging individuals to embrace the transient nature of worldly attachments as a form of sacrifice, freeing oneself from the shackles of material possessions. Aurelius emphasizes that "nothing should be done without purpose," advocating for intentionality in actions. Transcendental sacrifice, in this context, involves infusing purpose into every endeavor, aligning deeds with a higher calling or moral imperative.

Aurelius further encourages a minimalist approach to life by asserting that "most of what we say and do is unnecessary." Transcendental sacrifice, in this instance, involves shedding the superfluous—material, emotional, or intellectual—to make room for what truly matters. The Stoic belief in the attainability of human goals is evident in the assertion that if anything is humanly possible it lies within our reach, even if it may be hard to achieve. Transcendental sacrifice, as implied here, involves overcoming challenges and persisting in the face of difficulty, sacrificing immediate comfort to pursue enduring goals.

Aurelius deems it "disgraceful if, in this life where your body does not fail, your soul should fail first." This belief underscores the importance of maintaining moral integrity and spiritual resilience. In this context, transcendental sacrifice involves prioritizing the soul's well-being over fleeting bodily comforts or external successes, reflecting a commitment to enduring values. The transformative power of thoughts on one's character is highlighted by the assertion that "your mind will take on the character of your most frequent thoughts." In mental discipline, transcendental sacrifice involves sacrificing negative thought patterns for a mindset aligned with virtue and wisdom.

In the final quote, Aurelius suggests that one "lives with the gods who consistently shows them his soul content with its lot." This reflects the ultimate form of transcendental sacrifice—aligning one's soul with a higher, divine purpose. Sacrificing personal desires and ego for a harmonious existence with the divine encapsulates the Stoic ideal of living following the universal order, sacrificing individual will for a higher, transcendent purpose. Essentially, Aurelius's *Meditations* provide a rich tapestry of reflections embodying the spirit of transcendental sacrifice, urging individuals to elevate their lives through intentional, purpose-driven, and virtuous choices.

The provided passages present a conceptualization of the Übermensch through the lens of Marcus Aurelius' *Meditations*, Stoic philosophy, and Christ-like virtues. The Übermensch, in this context, embodies a person who transcends the ordinary human condition by adhering to a set of virtues and principles that elevate one's existence beyond immediate desires and fleeting pleasures. As suggested above, the prime motive of the Stoic Übermensch is not pursuing external power, as Nietzsche's Übermensch might suggest, but rather an internal quest for virtue, wisdom, and ethical conduct. The Stoic Übermensch described here draws inspiration from Marcus Aurelius, who focused on the inner realm of personal virtue and ethical principles rather than external dominance despite being a Roman Emperor.

The morality of this knightly-aristocratic version of the Übermensch is rooted in Stoic and Christ-like virtues, encompassing justice, chastity, fortitude, temperance, prudence, charity, hope, love, gratitude, and forgiveness. The Stoic Übermensch's moral compass is guided by a commitment to these virtues, reflecting a timeless exploration of ethical principles and the human condition. Transcendental sacrifice plays a central role in the teleology of this Übermensch, as evident in the Stoic emphasis on embracing change, purposeful action, minimalism, overcoming challenges, maintaining moral integrity, and aligning one's soul with a higher, divine purpose. The Stoic Übermensch's journey involves sacrificing the transient and superfluous for enduring values, pursuing a life of virtue and wisdom that contributes to humanity's common benefit and harmony. In essence, the teleology of this Übermensch revolves around the cultivation of a meaningful and purposeful existence through the embodiment of timeless virtues and the transformative power of transcendental sacrifice.

If will to truth is will to power, and power is acquired by sacrificing oneself to one's future self or a higher power (whether an Übermensch or God), then will to power is will to sacrifice, which is also the truth. Thus, the sixth angel goes and pours out his bowl on the earth. Next, we'll turn to the Bible, comparing and contrasting our last six iterations of the Übermensch to St. Michael the Archangel. We will aim to answer the following rhetorical question:

Who is like God?

CHAPTER TEN

Seventh Revelation: Who is like God?

The seventh angel, one who is like God, blows his trumpet. Revelation 12:7-9 (RSV): "Now war arose in heaven, Michael and his angels fighting against the dragon; and the dragon and his angels fought, but they were defeated and there was no longer any place for them in heaven. And the great dragon was thrown down, that ancient serpent, who is called the Devil and Satan, the deceiver of the whole world—he was thrown down to the earth, and his angels were thrown down with him."

So we pray to St. Michael:

Blessed Michael, the archangel, defend us in the hour of conflict.
Be our safeguard against the wickedness and snares of the devil
(may God restrain him, we humbly pray):
and do thou, O Prince of the heavenly host,
by the power of God thrust Satan down to hell
and with him those other wicked spirits
who wander through the world for the ruin of souls.
Amen.

St. Michael the Archangel, a celestial figure of immense significance in Judeo-Christian tradition, reveals himself as a symbol of divine protection, spiritual warfare, and transcendental sacrifice. Throughout the pages of the Bible, his appearances and interventions resonate with themes of cosmic battles, heavenly authority, and unwavering devotion to the divine purpose.

"Michael" originates in Hebrew, meaning "Who is like God?" This rhetorical question encapsulates a profound theological assertion, emphasizing the unparalleled nature of the Almighty. As an archangel, Michael is a celestial warrior and defender, embodying qualities that mirror divine majesty and power.

Merging the Übermensch with St. Michael, we will compare and contrast quotes depicting previous iterations of the Übermensch with scripture relating to St. Micael in the Bible. We will then reach a final conclusion, aiming to answer the ultimate question: Who is like God?

Biblical Depictions Of St. Michael

- Daniel 10:13 (RSV): "The prince of the kingdom of Persia withstood me twenty-one days; but Michael, one of the chief princes, came to help me, so I left him there with the prince of the kingdom of Persia."

Michael's intervention on behalf of the angel facing resistance from a prince of the Persian kingdom showcases his role as a powerful defender. His timely assistance reflects the virtue of selfless aid, akin to Christ's sacrifice for humanity. Michael's actions embody the transcendental sacrifice of intervening in the cosmic struggle between good and evil, demonstrating that the divine principle of protection is inherent in answering "Who is like God?"

- Daniel 12:1 (RSV): "At that time shall arise Michael, the great prince who has charge of your people. And there shall be a time of trouble, such as never has been since there was a nation till that time; but at that time your people shall be delivered, every one whose name shall be found written in the book."

Michael is depicted as the great prince who arises to

protect God's people during a time of unprecedented distress. This emphasizes his role as a savior and guardian. The verse underscores the transcendental sacrifice of shielding the faithful during challenging times, mirroring Christ's redemptive mission. The question "Who is like God?" finds resonance in Michael's sacrificial protection, aligning with the virtues associated with Christ.

- Jude 1:9 (RSV): "But when the archangel Michael, contending with the devil, disputed about the body of Moses, he did not presume to pronounce a reviling judgment upon him, but said, 'The Lord rebuke you.'"

The episode of Michael refraining from condemning the devil but invoking the Lord's rebuke demonstrates a profound humility and refusal to engage in baseless condemnation. This reflects Christ-like virtue, emphasizing mercy over judgment. Michael's stance resonates with the transcendental sacrifice of forgiveness, answering "Who is like God?" by embodying divine mercy and restraint.

- Revelation 12:7-9 (RSV): "Now war arose in heaven, Michael and his angels fighting against the dragon; and the dragon and his angels fought, but they were defeated and there was no longer any place for them in heaven. And the great dragon was thrown down, that ancient serpent, who is called the Devil and Satan, the deceiver of the whole world—he was thrown down to the earth, and his angels were thrown down with him."

This passage describes the celestial war where Michael and his angels defeat the dragon. The victorious struggle against evil echoes Christ's triumph over sin and the forces of darkness. Michael's role in this cosmic battle signifies a commitment to justice and righteousness, reflecting the divine question "Who is like God?" in the context of moral victory.

- Revelation 12:10 (RSV): "And I heard a loud voice in heaven, saying, 'Now the salvation and the power and the kingdom of our God and the authority of his Christ have come, for the accuser of our brethren has been thrown down, who accuses them day and night before our God.'"

The proclamation of salvation, power, and God's kingdom associates Michael with these divine attributes. His role in silencing the accuser aligns with Christ's redemptive work. Michael's actions embody the answer to "Who is like God?" by demonstrating the authority and power of the divine over accusations and injustice.

- 1 Thessalonians 4:16 (RSV): "For the Lord himself will descend from heaven with a cry of command, with the archangel's call, and with the sound of the trumpet of God. And the dead in Christ will rise first."

The mention of the archangel's voice accompanying the Lord's return connects Michael to the eschatological narrative. This emphasizes his role in the divine plan for the resurrection, showcasing a Christ-like virtue of participating in the ultimate redemption of believers. The question "Who is like God?" is reflected in Michael's involvement in the triumphant return of the Lord.

- Revelation 12:12 (RSV): "Rejoice then, O heaven and you that dwell therein! But woe to you, O earth and sea, for the devil has come down to you in great wrath, because he knows that his time is short!"

Michael's role in the heavenly rejoicing and the impending woe on earth highlights his dual nature as a warrior and a protector. The awareness of the devil's fury and limited time echoes Christ's warnings about the adversary. The question "Who is like God?" resonates as Michael prepares to confront and overcome the forces of darkness.

- Daniel 10:21 (RSV): "But I will tell you what is inscribed in the book of truth: there is none who contends by my side against these except Michael, your prince."

Michael's support in the Book of Truth emphasizes his unique role in divine revelation and guidance. This role aligns with Christ as the embodiment of divine truth. "Who is like God?" is addressed as Michael aligning with the divine order and purpose revealed in the Book of Truth, an alignment that mirrors syzygy.

- Revelation 19:11-14 (RSV): "Then I saw heaven opened, and behold, a white horse! He who sat upon it is called Faithful and True, and in righteousness he judges and makes war. His eyes are like a flame of fire, and on his head are many diadems; and he has a name inscribed which no one knows but himself. He is clad in a robe dipped in[a] blood, and the name by which he is called is The Word of God. And the armies of heaven, arrayed in fine linen, white and pure, followed him on white horses."

Although not explicitly mentioning Michael, this passage describes a rider on a white horse, embodying justice and truth. While traditionally associated with Christ, the virtues depicted align with the overarching theme of divine justice and righteousness. The question "Who is like God?" echoes in the portrayal of a figure wielding unparalleled authority and righteousness.

- Hebrews 1:14 (RSV): "Are they not all ministering spirits sent forth to serve, for the sake of those who are to obtain salvation?"

This verse emphasizes the role of angels as ministering spirits sent to serve those who will inherit salvation. While not directly mentioning Michael, it aligns with his protective and supportive role, reflecting Christ-like virtues of service and care for the redeemed. The question "Who is like God?" is implicit in the shared mission of angels, including Michael, to serve the divine purpose of salvation.

As derived from the Bible, this less literal version of the Übermensch can be characterized by a teleology centered around divine virtues, protection, and transcendental sacrifice —qualities embodied by the Archangel Michael in the biblical texts. Michael is a powerful defender, intervening selflessly in cosmic struggles and protecting God's people during distress. This Übermensch, aligning with Michael's virtues, would prioritize selfless aid, sacrificial protection, and guardianship as prime motives. Morality for this Übermensch would be intricately tied to divine principles, echoing the question of his namesake: "Who is like God?" The Übermensch's morality would involve emulating the virtues associated with Michael—justice, humility, forgiveness, and a commitment to divine truth.

Transcendental sacrifice plays a central role in the teleology of this Übermensch. Michael's interventions in celestial battles, protection of the faithful, and participation in eschatological events signify a willingness to sacrifice personal comfort and safety for the greater good. The Übermensch, inspired by Michael's example, would embrace a life of purpose and intentional action, recognizing that true virtue involves transcending personal desires and aligning with a higher, divine order. The Übermensch's moral framework, shaped by divine principles and marked by transcendental sacrifice, seeks to answer the ultimate question by striving to mirror the virtues associated with the divine and contributing to the cosmic struggle between good and evil. Ultimately, such an Übermensch would eagerly and willingly confront the greatest evil of all—Satan—without regard for himself.

These biblical passages offer glimpses into the multifaceted role of St. Michael, portraying him as a warrior, a protector, and a herald of divine justice. The overarching theme of transcendental sacrifice is woven into his celestial battles against the forces of evil, reflecting a commitment to the cosmic order and the salvation of God's people. As we delve into the scriptures, we unravel the profound significance of St. Michael the Archangel, whose name resounds with the eternal question: Who is like God?

Reflections Of Who Is Like God

Let's sample our previous knightly-aristocratic iterations of the Übermensch, drawing parallels between them and St. Michael. By doing so, we will clearly and definitively refute Nietzsche's philosophy by arriving back at the reflection of God despite following his recommendations to the contrary.

These quotes highlight transcendental sacrifice and answer the question, "Who is like God?" Additionally, they demonstrate without question that morality cannot exist without God.

- "I know I hung on a wind-battered tree nine long nights, pierced by a spear and given to Odin, myself onto myself, on that tree whose roots grow in a place no one has ever seen. No one gave me food, no one gave me drink. At the end I peered down, I took the runes—screaming, I took them—and then I fell."

In this excerpt from the *Hávamál*, a profound symbol of transcendental sacrifice emerges, asking the question, "Who is like God?" The act of hanging on a tree for nine nights signifies a transformative experience, accompanied by the piercing of a spear and the acquisition of runes, hinting at a divine ordeal and sacred knowledge. This sacrificial theme resonates with biblical representations of St. Michael engaging in cosmic battles. The passage underscores sacrifice's solitary and divine nature, emphasizing that morality and transcendent knowledge stem from divine revelation. It suggests a connection with the divine as the source of true understanding and virtue. This knightly-aristocratic version of the Übermensch, inspired by the *Hávamál*, centers on transcendental sacrifice, divine revelation, and the pursuit of sacred knowledge, highlighting a deep connection with the divine. The Übermensch's teleological aim involves transcending human limitations through trials and solitary ordeals to acquire sacred wisdom. Morality is intrinsically tied to divine principles, emphasizing a direct connection with the sacred. Transcendental sacrifice is a cornerstone of the Übermensch's teleology, mirroring the *Hávamál's* imagery. Inspired by St. Michael's teleology, the Übermensch's quest for sacred knowledge may be more individualistic and focused on personal communion with the divine, addressing "Who is like God?" by embodying transformative aspects of divine sacrifice.

- "While on the Way, do not begrudge death."

Within the *Book of Five Rings*, a profound quote

encapsulates the idea of transcendental sacrifice, echoing biblical representations of St. Michael and emphasizing the intimate connection between morality and the divine. Rooted in the concept of the "Way," or the path of life and virtue, the passage encourages a mindset that surpasses the fear of death in the pursuit of higher principles. This aligns with the biblical portrayal of St. Michael engaging in celestial battles for the divine order. The Eastern philosophy of the "Way" parallels the righteousness and moral order associated with divine will in biblical narratives. The quote's emphasis on not begrudging death implies that true morality, honor, and virtue often demand a willingness to sacrifice one's life for a higher cause, highlighting the intrinsic link between true morality and transcendental sacrifice to a higher, divine order. In a knightly-aristocratic version of the Übermensch inspired by *The Book of Five Rings*, teleology is deeply rooted in transcendental sacrifice, promoting the pursuit of the "Way" without fear of death. This Übermensch is motivated by a relentless commitment to higher principles, moral excellence, and a dedication to the divine, paralleling the sacrificial ethos of St. Michael's cosmic battles for the divine order. Transcendental sacrifice remains central in the teleology of this Übermensch, fostering a mindset that rises above the fear of death in the pursuit of higher principles. The quest for the "Way" inherently involves a readiness to sacrifice personal well-being for the greater good, sharing similarities with St. Michael's sacrificial ethos. While both are committed to transcendental sacrifice and divine alignment, the specific path and focus of this Übermensch may differ, reflecting the unique philosophical context of *The Book of Five Rings*.

- "All warfare is based on deception."

Sun Tzu's philosophy, captured in this quote, mirrors the qualities of transcendental sacrifice and addresses the divine connection in biblical representations of St. Michael. The quote highlights the inherent sacrifice in warfare, where strategic deception serves a higher purpose, contrasting with the opposite implication (that all peace is rooted in truth).

As a celestial warrior, St. Michael embodies virtue in cosmic battles against evil. The notion that warfare involves deception aligns with the strategic wisdom in biblical conflicts, suggesting that moral decisions, even in war, are guided by a deeper understanding of divine principles. Essentially, the quote implies that true morality, even in the harsh realities of warfare, relies on a connection to divine wisdom. In a knightly-aristocratic version of the Übermensch inspired by Sun Tzu, teleology centers on strategic wisdom, transcendental sacrifice, and a profound link to divine principles. This Übermensch strategically pursues higher purposes, mirroring Sun Tzu's emphasis on using deception for a greater cause, with morality intricately tied to a divine framework akin to St. Michael's battles. Transcendental sacrifice remains central, reflected in the strategic use of deception for higher goals, aligning with St. Michael's celestial battles. However, the approach may differ, emphasizing strategic wisdom in the context of war and offering a nuanced perspective on the interplay between morality, sacrifice, and divine principles.

- "A man of high purpose and a man with deep humaneness would not seek to stay alive at the expense of humaneness. There are times when they would sacrifice their lives to have humaneness fulfilled."

As captured in this quote, Confucius's perspective mirrors transcendental sacrifice, resonates with the celestial virtues embodied by figures like St. Michael, and suggests that morality is inseparable from a connection to the divine. The idea of sacrificing one's life for humaneness aligns with the selflessness often associated with celestial beings like St. Michael in cosmic battles against evil. The quote emphasizes that high purpose and humaneness are intertwined with transcendent principles, implying that true virtue and morality are rooted in the divine. In a knightly-aristocratic version of the Übermensch inspired by Confucius, teleology centers on virtuous living, selflessness, and pursuing a high purpose, echoing St. Michael's cosmic battles. The Übermensch's commitment to moral excellence is intimately linked to the divine, reflecting a deep understanding that true virtue stems from transcendent principles. Transcendental sacrifice remains central, exemplified by the willingness to sacrifice one's life for noble causes, echoing St. Michael's sacrificial ethos yet introducing a nuanced perspective through Confucian ideals.

- "For the Romans did in these cases what all wise princes should do, who consider not only present but also future discords and diligently guard against them; for being foreseen they can easily be remedied, but if one waits till they are at hand, the medicine is no longer in time as the malady has become incurable; it happening with this as with those hectic fevers, as doctors say, which at their beginning are easy to cure but difficult to recognize, but in course of time when they have not at first been recognized and treated, become easy to recognize and difficult to cure."

Niccolò Machiavelli intricately weaves together the concepts of transcendental sacrifice, the query "Who is like God?", biblical echoes of St. Michael, and the assertion that morality requires a connection to God. The passage underscores the importance of foresight and strategic planning for virtuous action, suggesting that sacrificing present comforts for a higher purpose aligns with transcendental sacrifice. It implies that moral decisions rooted in divine principles often involve sacrificing immediate benefits to prevent future harm, akin to the strategic battles of angels like St. Michael. In a knightly-aristocratic Übermensch inspired by Machiavelli, teleology centers on wisdom, strategic foresight, and the willingness to make present sacrifices to avert future discord. This Übermensch, committed to effective leadership, recognizes the intimate link between morality and the divine, echoing the celestial battles of St. Michael. Transcendental sacrifice is pivotal, emphasizing enduring immediate challenges for a higher purpose, with a unique focus on foresight to prevent future issues. Both Machiavelli's Übermensch and St. Michael share a strategic approach, emphasizing pragmatism and addressing potential issues before escalation, which introduces a distinctive aspect, echoing divine guidance and transcendent principles.

- "He lives with the gods who consistently shows them his soul content with its lot, performing the wishes of that divinity, that fragment of himself which Zeus has given each person to guard and guide him. In each of us this divinity is our mind and reason."

Marcus Aurelius's quote from *Meditations* exemplifies transcendental sacrifice, echoing the biblical representation of St. Michael and addressing the question, "Who is like God?" It encapsulates the Stoic idea of aligning one's soul with a higher purpose, sacrificing personal desires, and finding contentment in one's fate. The mention of Zeus and the divine spark within individuals aligns with the notion of recognizing a transcendent power. The emphasis on moral alignment with this internal divinity suggests that true virtue stems from a connection to a higher, transcendent order. This Stoic Übermensch, inspired by Marcus Aurelius, centers on harmonizing with the gods, finding contentment, and sacrificing personal desires for a harmonious existence guided by a moral compass rooted in a connection to the divine. Transcendental sacrifice is key, mirroring the Stoic idea of relinquishing individual whims for moral alignment with a higher authority. While resonating with St. Michael's sacrificial virtues, this Stoic-inspired teleology adds a nuanced focus on inner alignment and tranquility as integral components of virtuous living.

These selected quotes collectively capture themes of sacrifice, virtue, wisdom, and strategic thinking, resonating with the virtues associated with St. Michael and addressing the question "Who is like God?" in various aspects of human experience and divine understanding. That question is a weapon—a flaming arrow, like the flaming sword that guards the Tree of Life—designed by God to defeat Satan with the Word.

- Genesis 3:22-24 (RSV): "Then the Lord God said, 'Behold, the man has become like one of us, knowing good and evil;

and now, lest he put forth his hand and take also of the tree of life, and eat, and live for ever'—therefore the Lord God sent him forth from the garden of Eden, to till the ground from which he was taken. He drove out the man; and at the east of the garden of Eden he placed the cherubim, and a flaming sword which turned every way, to guard the way to the tree of life."

So, who is like God? If will to truth is will to power, and power is acquired by sacrificing oneself to one's future self or a higher power (whether an Übermensch or God), then will to power is will to sacrifice, which is also God's truth. At this point, the answer should be abundantly clear. You are like God, made in His image. So am I, aiming toward God. So are we all, as reflections of the Holy Trinity. We are a syzygy connected by divine truth. So is every conception of the knightly-aristocratic Übermensch; therefore, God is *not* dead!

Thus, the seventh angel goes and pours out his bowl on the earth. Revelation 19:20 (RSV): "And the beast was captured, and with it the false prophet who in its presence had worked the signs by which he deceived those who had received the mark of the beast and those who worshiped its image. These two were thrown alive into the lake of fire that burns with sulphur."

CHAPTER ELEVEN

Syzygy Conquers Schism

How do we define truth? Is it distinct from or wholly integrated with natural law? Is it transcendent? Is it divine? More importantly, how do we define God? These questions are incredibly challenging to answer, possibly infinitely complex. Nevertheless, let's not quit before the attempt as we complete an indestructible argument against Nietzsche's will to power. That argument should be rooted firmly in God's divine truth and wisdom.

First, we will investigate the nature of truth from scientific, religious, and philosophical perspectives, identifying the flaws and misconceptions conceived from each. Specifically, we will analyze truth obtained through sensation and observation, empiricism, and Cartesian dualism as it compares to reasoned (logos) or divine (Christian Logos) discourse. We will then attempt to reconcile these dual *a priori* and *a posteriori* perspectives using logic, ultimately utilizing that integrated framework to further disprove the philosophy of Friedrich Nietzsche.

To begin, we'll identify natural laws from the realm of physics, from classical and quantum mechanics. Conclusions drawn from these natural laws will be analyzed through the lens of Cartesian dualism. Then, we'll compare those observations to their reflections in pre-Christian reasoned discourse, coined "logos" by ancient Greek philosophers. In addition to elements of Nietzsche's philosophy, we will look at other Eastern and Western worldviews that mirror our working philosophical framework. After that, we will contrast the logos of ancient philosophers to the divine Word, the Christian Logos. Lastly, we'll tie it all together with a nice bow, calling upon C. S. Lewis's "Argument from Reason," Gödel's ontological proof of God, and the Cognitive-Theoretic Model of the Universe (CTMU). While controversial, Chris Langan introduced the latter as a novel metaphysical and philosophical theory in the early 2000s.

Classical And Quantum Mechanics

So, what does physics offer us regarding the truth? Three laws of thermodynamics—not including the zeroth law—apply to classical and quantum mechanics:

1. Energy cannot be created or destroyed.
2. For a spontaneous process, the universe's entropy increases.
3. A perfect crystal at zero Kelvin has zero entropy.

The first law of thermodynamics establishes that energy cannot be created or destroyed in an isolated system; it can only change forms. The total energy of a system and its surroundings remains constant. This law is often expressed as the equation $\Delta U = Q - W$, where ΔU is the change in internal energy, Q is the heat added to the system, and W is the work done by the system. Essentially, the first law emphasizes energy conservation and its ability to transfer between different forms within a closed system.

The second law of thermodynamics explains the concept of entropy, which measures the disorder or randomness in a system. In any energy transfer or transformation, the potential energy of the state will always be less than that of the initial state if no energy enters or leaves the system. This law is often associated with the idea that natural processes tend to move towards greater disorder or entropy. One common expression of the second law is that heat always flows spontaneously from hot to cold regions.

The third law of thermodynamics establishes that as the temperature of a system approaches absolute zero (0 Kelvin or -273.15 degrees Celsius), the system's entropy approaches a minimum value. In other words, it becomes highly ordered and reaches a state of perfect crystalline order. This law is crucial for understanding the behavior of matter at very low temperatures. It helps explain why absolute zero is considered an unattainable temperature.

Quantum mechanics also gives us a series of counterintuitive or even paradoxical principles:

1. The Uncertainty Principle
2. The Observer Effect
3. Quantum Superposition (symbolized by Schrödinger's Cat)
4. Zero-point Energy

The *uncertainty principle*, formulated by Werner Heisenberg, states that it is impossible to know a particle's position and momentum (or velocity) simultaneously and precisely. The more accurately you measure one of these properties, the less accurately you can know the other. This inherent uncertainty is fundamental to quantum mechanics. It challenges classical notions of determinism and predictability on a microscopic scale.

The *observer effect* refers to the idea that the act of observation or measurement can influence the state of a quantum system. In quantum mechanics, the state of a particle is often described by a probability wave until it is observed, at which point the wave collapses, and the particle assumes a definite state. The observer effect highlights the role of consciousness or measurement devices in the behavior of quantum systems, raising philosophical questions about the nature of reality and the observer's impact on it.

Several key experiments influenced the formulation of the observer effect in quantum mechanics. One of the pioneering experiments was the double-slit experiment, where particles, such as electrons, exhibited wave-like interference patterns when unobserved and particle-like behavior when observed. This result suggested that the act of observation or measurement influenced the behavior of the particles. Additionally, the delayed-choice quantum eraser experiment demonstrated that the observer's decision to measure or not measure the path of a particle could retroactively affect its behavior, even after the particle had passed through the experimental apparatus. These experiments, among others, contributed to the formulation of the observer effect, emphasizing the fundamental role of observation in shaping the behavior and properties of quantum systems.

Quantum superposition is a principle that allows quantum particles to exist in multiple states simultaneously. Unlike classical particles, which exist in well-defined states, quantum particles can exist in a superposition of states until a measurement is made. This means that, for example, an electron can be in multiple positions or spin states simultaneously. Superposition is fundamental to developing quantum computers, which leverage this property to perform parallel computations.

Schrödinger's Cat is a thought experiment proposed by Erwin Schrödinger to illustrate the concept of superposition. In the scenario, a cat is placed in a sealed box with a radioactive atom and a vial of poison. If the atom decays, the poison is released, and the cat dies. If it doesn't decay, the cat survives. According to quantum mechanics, before the box is opened and the system is observed, the cat exists in a superposition of being both alive and dead. Only when the box is opened and observed is the cat's state determined. Schrödinger's Cat is often used to highlight the strange and counterintuitive aspects of quantum superposition and the role of observation in collapsing quantum states.

In classical physics, the concept of "absolute zero energy," or a system at a state of "zero energy," is somewhat theoretical. The idea of absolute zero temperature, where a system would have minimal energy, is a theoretical limit defined in the Kelvin temperature scale. At absolute zero (0 Kelvin or -273.15 degrees Celsius), classical physics suggests a system would have minimal thermal motion and no heat energy.

However, in quantum mechanics, even at absolute zero, particles are still subject to *zero-point energy*, which is the lowest possible energy in a quantum mechanical physical system. This arises due to the inherent uncertainty in the position and momentum of particles described by Heisenberg's uncertainty principle. Therefore, achieving a state of truly zero energy is not practically attainable in the quantum realm.

In experimental physics, reaching absolute zero is extremely challenging. Scientists have been able to approach temperatures very close to absolute zero using techniques such as laser cooling and evaporative cooling. These experiments involve removing energy from a system. Still, it's important to note that achieving exactly zero energy remains a theoretical concept.

For the sake of brevity, we've committed a paragraph or two to a discussion of each law or principle and no more. In that regard, you're encouraged to investigate them further independently, especially considering I'm not a physicist capable of fully articulating their nuances. Therefore, take the following conclusions with a massive grain of salt. Draw your own conclusions, and see if you agree. Here are mine drawn by integrating these laws and principles:

1. The Ontology of Entropy: Nature consists of energy that transforms from substance to substance; that energy is indestructible, but its form dissolves and transforms *ad nauseam*.

2. The Epistemology of Entropy: We cannot observe all of nature with certainty due to this perpetual and irreversible thermodynamic equilibrium that creates uncertainty between the manifestation and transformation of observable substances, the influences of observation and measurement on

quantum states, and the existence of (pre-conscious) quantum superposition beyond conscious perception. Thus, since conscious observation alone is paradoxically a source of uncertainty, true thermodynamic equilibrium is unknowable outside of a conscious-unconscious duality, which possibly becomes transcendent by aligning with a pre-conscious state to form a syzygy. Otherwise, nature epistemologically becomes imbalanced or irrational through singularly conscious or unconscious observation.

3. The Teleology of Entropy: Heat always flows from greater to lesser due to entropy, constantly propelling observable substances along unpredictable paths once observed, and, thus, we can only connect arrow and target, cause and effect, by focusing our observation on the underlying aim—the energy and not the form.

4. The Metaphysical Syntax (Syntactic Operator) of Entropy: Nature becomes imbalanced and irrational through universal quantum waveform collapse (observation) without entropy, simultaneously becoming all substance and no energy. This pure crystalline substance does not exist except as a metaphysical form or barrier beyond which conscious observation cannot penetrate, according to the epistemology of entropy, and, thus, nature re-equilibrates *ad nauseam* before ever reaching this boundary. Therein lies the self-resolving paradox, a syzygy of ontology and epistemology aligned through the interaction of teleology and syntactic operators.

The latter conclusion was arrived at by the following thought experiment: combining the scenario described in the third law of thermodynamics with Schrödinger's Cat. We'll call it *Schrödinger's Crystal*. More than a physical reality, it's a metaphysical syntactic boundary that contains the ontology of entropy through teleological feedback and epistemology, guiding heat like an arrow to an ever-moving target using a language of perfect forms that don't exist.

In a perfect crystal at 0 Kelvin (absolute zero), according to the third law of thermodynamics, the entropy of the crystal would theoretically approach zero. This means the crystal would be in its lowest energy state. At such low temperatures, particles would come to a standstill.

This principle does not apply to quantum states and particles regarding quantum superposition. Without observation or measurement, particles can exist in multiple states simultaneously. If we apply these principles to a perfect crystal at 0 K, where entropy is minimized, and molecular motion nearly ceases, it implies that the quantum states of the particles within the crystal could still exist in a superposition of states. Once observed, however, Heisenberg's uncertainty principle applies.

In practical terms, this suggests that at 0 K and without observation, particles within the crystal could simultaneously exist in various quantum states. The lack of thermal energy (temperature) and the absence of observation would allow this perfect crystal to exist in a quantum superposition, potentially representing a scenario where the particles are rigidly locked into a single state within the crystal lattice while simultaneously in a state of all possibilities. Furthermore, even with observation, the uncertainty principle tells us that zero energy is practically unattainable due to residual zero-point energy. It's important to note that this interpretation is within the realm of quantum mechanics and relies on the theoretical aspects of superposition and the third law of thermodynamics. Actual observations and experiments at such extreme conditions are highly challenging and approach the limits of current scientific understanding.

So, what happens to a pure crystal at 0 Kelvin without entropy or an observer to collapse the quantum waveform? If Schrödinger's Crystal represents the lowest possible thermal energy, and if the laws of thermodynamics and quantum mechanics apply, then how can it be both no entropy and all possibility? Can this phenomenon even be empirically studied? Do quantum mechanics even apply under these circumstances? If so, wouldn't that make Schrödinger's Crystal all substance in a single state, including all possibilities in multiple states, and, therefore, no single state simultaneously, a substanceless substance? But wait, how does one observe nothing, resulting in something?

On the flip side, if Schrödinger's Crystal becomes observed, how can the observation of all possibilities result in a perfect configuration absent possibility with zero-point energy? Shouldn't a perfect form without possibilities have no residual energy, according to the third law of thermodynamics? I'll leave that one up to the physicists to flesh out; I'm not ashamed to admit when I don't have the brainpower. However, Schrödinger's Crystal appears less physical than metaphysical, operating as a syntactic boundary of impossibly perfect crystalline forms that guide entropy through the teleology of heat without violating its ontology or epistemology. Said differently, perhaps Schrödinger's Crystal communicates as a meta-language with the teleology of heat to contain the ontology and epistemology of entropy. Now, we should unpack these ideas a little further to provide further clarity:

1. Nature as Transformative Energy: The notion that nature is fundamentally composed of energy undergoing continuous transformation aligns with principles in physics. According to this perspective, the various forms and substances in the natural world are expressions of this underlying, persistent energy.

2. Indestructible Energy, Transient Substance: Describing energy as indestructible implies a continuity that transcends the transient nature of physical substances. This aligns with the conservation of energy principle, a foundational concept in physics stating that energy is neither created nor destroyed but merely changes forms.

3. Observation and Thermodynamic Equilibrium: The assertion that we cannot observe all of nature with certainty due to a perpetual and irreversible thermodynamic equilibrium introduces a crucial idea. In thermodynamics, equilibrium represents a state of balance, and the irreversible nature of processes reflects the inexorable march toward disorder or entropy. The acknowledgment that this perpetual equilibrium constrains observation underscores the inherent limitations in our ability to comprehend the entirety of the natural world.

4. Entropy and Unpredictable Paths: The reference to entropy and heat flow from greater to lesser underscores the idea that natural processes tend toward increased disorder. This aligns with the second law of thermodynamics, emphasizing the irreversible nature of certain transformations. The concept of unpredictable paths following observation suggests a dynamic and evolving reality shaped by the thermodynamic arrow of time.

5. Connecting Arrow and Target through Aim: The metaphorical use of arrows and targets highlights the challenge of establishing deterministic connections between observed phenomena. Focusing on the underlying aim, represented by energy rather than substance, implies a shift from a deterministic worldview to one where the fundamental essence is sought beyond the particulars of observed forms.

6. Equilibrium through Conscious-Unconscious Syzygy: Introducing the concept of equilibrium through syzygy adds a layer of complexity. Superposition, a quantum mechanical principle, suggests that particles can exist in multiple states simultaneously. Connecting this to equilibrium implies a delicate balance between refinement and less substantial states. The role of conscious observation as a

source of unpredictability introduces the idea that a balance between conscious and unconscious modes of observation is essential for wholly perceiving the natural world. This raises an extreme yet profound question: do humans comprehend nature through parallel conscious and unconscious processes to optimize their natural harmony, and does using only one singular, linear process, therefore, lead to disharmony?

7. Nature's Chaotic Potential: The statement that nature becomes imbalanced and irrational through singularly conscious or unconscious observation implies that an exclusive focus on either conscious or unconscious modes of observation disrupts the delicate equilibrium and introduces chaos, inversion, and division. This underscores the importance of balance and integration in understanding the complexities of nature.

So, nature reveals itself like a Chinese finger trap; the harder you look, the less you see the big picture. Relax a little bit, and the imminent truth reveals itself. Cause and effect are bound only by energy; arrow and target are connected only by aim. To hit the mark consistently, you must always aim. On rare occasions, fortune aims for you, but if you hit the mark in that way, without aim, you will rarely hit it consistently. This metaphor highlights teleological causation. More importantly, nature is either totally imbalanced and irrational as a singularity of a fragmented mind, fragmented by unintended consequences, or totally balanced and rational as a harmonious syzygy of a conscious-unconscious mind, which becomes whole by mirrored intention. Therefore, a syzygy of energy—conscious and unconscious, mind and body, Word and flesh—must aim two arrows in harmony to strike the bullseye of God's truth.

Is God reflected in conscious-unconscious syzygy as *telic synchronicity*—divine meaning derived from simultaneous events, which appear significantly related but have no obvious discernable cause otherwise?

Truth emerging from syzygy as telic synchronicity seems quite radical, a fusion of Carl Jung's concepts of syzygy and synchronicity and Chris Langan's *telic recursion*, all of which we will detail toward the end of this chapter. Monotheism from dualism seems even more so, possibly a biased conclusion tainted by a flawed interpretation of natural law. If not a misinterpretation, however, it is broken only to the degree that natural law is broken by its own logic.

Cartesian Dualism

To provide a comprehensive understanding, let's first define Cartesian dualism, highlighting René Descartes' philosophy, and then draw connections with the notion of truth emerging from conscious-unconscious syzygy through telic synchronicity. Cartesian dualism, proposed by René Descartes, is a philosophical concept that postulates the existence of two fundamental substances: the mind (or soul) and the body. According to Descartes, the mind and body are distinct entities with different natures. The mind is non-material, thinking, and conscious. At the same time, the body is a mechanical material that operates according to unconscious physical laws. This dualistic view suggests a separation between mental and physical phenomena, between consciousness and unconsciousness.

Descartes' philosophy laid the foundation for Cartesian dualism by famously expressing "Cogito, ergo sum" (I think, therefore I am), emphasizing the certainty of one's existence as a thinking being. Descartes believed in an incorporeal mind that interacts with the physical body. While he acknowledged the interaction between mind and body, the dualism arises from the distinction in their essential natures.

Truth emerging from telic synchronicity offers a different perspective, suggesting a conscious-unconscious syzygy within nature that contemplates its sanity or insanity.

It presupposes that nature is either fragmented and irrational or harmonious and rational, reflecting God in the latter state. Condensed into an axiom, using the famous expression Descartes gave us, one might rephrase it accordingly: "God thinks, therefore I am, but I am in Hell if I don't aim for that truth; when I aim for that truth, I am like God." From this perspective, truth emerges from this syzygy by teleological causation, resulting in telic synchronicity.

Cartesian dualism, on the other hand, emphasizes a distinction between mind and body, focusing on the interaction between two separate substances. Both perspectives touch upon the concept of harmony. Cartesian dualism involves the interaction between mind and body, while our working philosophical framework emphasizes the necessity of synchronicity between conscious and unconscious elements, too, but more specifically in teleology. In other words, conscious-unconscious syzygy reflects God due to teleologic harmony; conscious-unconscious *schism* reflects Hell due to teleologic disharmony. Cartesian dualism doesn't explicitly connect the mind-body distinction to God's reflection; Descartes' philosophy is often associated with a mechanistic view of the physical world. Our current framework adds another layer to Cartesian dualism: the mind and body are either totally sane or insane, depending on the state of their relationship, whether discordant or harmonious in terms of teleology.

In summary, while Cartesian dualism concerns the separation of mind and body—their ontology—our working philosophical framework broadens the perspective to consider teleology. Both views involve the idea of harmony, but the context and implications differ. Thus, our current philosophical framework proposes that truth emerges as telic synchronicity from syzygy, emphasizing the need for balance and mirrored intention between conscious and unconscious aspects—mind and body, Word and flesh—in their will.

Theory Of Forms

Where else can we find a reflection of transcendental truth in conscious-unconscious syzygy, monotheism through dualism? Let's start with logos and examine reasoned human discourse across cultures and time. Representing Western philosophy, we'll start with Plato and Socrates.

As articulated through Socrates' dialogues, Plato's Theory of Forms represents a fundamental aspect of his philosophical framework. Central to this theory is the notion that the physical world we perceive is an imperfect and transient reflection of a higher, non-material realm of ideal Forms or Ideas. In Plato's dialogue *Phaedo*, Socrates argues that the material world is subject to change and impermanence. At the same time, the Forms are eternal and immutable, serving as the ultimate reality. This distinction between the visible, changing world and the transcendent world of Forms lays the foundation for Plato's epistemology and metaphysics.

Two critical aspects of Plato's Theory of Forms are participation and recollection, where individual instances in the physical world participate in or partake of the Forms. In *Parmenides*, Socrates states, "No, for it might be like day, which is one and the same, is in many places at once, and yet is not separated from itself; so each idea, though one and the same, might be in all its participants at once."

In *Meno*, after effectively demonstrating knowledge is not acquired but recollected by questioning a slave boy about geometry, he asks Meno, "Then he who does not know may still have true notions of that which he does not know?"

To this, Meno agrees. Their dialogue continues, coming to the point where the recollection, rather than acquisition, of knowledge supports the existence of an immortal soul.

"And if the truth of all things always existed in the soul, then the soul is immortal."

This participation and recollection provides a framework

for understanding the universal nature of Forms and their connection to particular instances in the empirical world, as well as an immortal soul.

So Meno says, "There again, Socrates, your words seem to me excellent."

Plato's Theory of Forms can be linked to broader discussions of monotheism through conscious-unconscious syzygy, especially when considering the transcendent nature of the Forms. While Plato's philosophy is not explicitly monotheistic, emphasizing a higher, unchanging reality implies a transcendence that resonates with certain monotheistic traditions. As eternal and perfect entities, the Forms share similarities with monotheism's concept of a singular, divine source. The dualistic nature of Plato's worldview, distinguishing between the world of appearances and the world of Forms, aligns with the dualistic tendencies often found in monotheistic theology, where there is a distinction between the divine and the material.

Moreover, Plato's Theory of Forms can be seen as contributing to the philosophical foundations that influenced later thinkers who grappled with monotheistic ideas. The transcendent, eternal nature of the Forms anticipates discussions within monotheistic traditions about the nature of an eternal, unchanging God. While Plato did not explicitly develop a monotheistic theology, the Theory of Forms laid the groundwork for exploring the relationship between the material world and a higher, transcendent reality. This theme resonates in later philosophical and religious discourse.

Taoism

Now, we'll shift focus to Eastern philosophy, where we'll merge our ever-expanding theory with the wisdom of Lao Tzu. Lao Tzu's *Tao Te Ching* is a foundational text of Taoism, presenting a philosophical and spiritual perspective rooted in the concept of the *Tao*. This ineffable and fundamental principle underlies and unites the universe. Central to Lao Tzu's teachings is the idea of *Wu Wei*, often translated as "non-action" or "effortless action."

Lao Tzu writes, "Therefore, the sage produces without possessing, acts without expectations, and accomplishes without abiding in her accomplishments."

Wu Wei is the art of spontaneous and natural action, aligning oneself with the flow of the Tao rather than resisting or forcing outcomes.

"Being and non-being produce each other."

Thus, Wu Wei can be reframed in a broader discussion of monotheism through conscious-unconscious syzygy by considering its implications for the relationship between the individual and the divine. In monotheistic traditions, there is often a dualistic tension between the individual will and the will of a singular, transcendent God. Lao Tzu's Wu Wei offers an alternative perspective, emphasizing a harmonious alignment with the Tao, representing a unifying and pervasive force akin to the divine.

Wu Wei suggests a different approach than Cartesian dualism, where conscious divinity and unconscious material are often distinct and in tension. Rather than seeing the divine as external and separate from the individual, Wu Wei implies an oneness with the Tao, aligning personal action with the universe's natural order. This aligns with the Taoist idea that the Tao is both immanent and transcendent, suggesting a monotheistic understanding of the relationship between the individual and the divine.

Lao Tzu's emphasis on spontaneity, simplicity, and the natural course of events challenges dualistic notions of a struggle between the individual and a separate divine will. "Therefore the sage grasps the one and becomes the model for all." Wu Wei invites a reevaluation of the relationship between the individual and the transcendent, proposing a way of being that harmonizes with the underlying unity of the Tao. While not explicitly monotheistic, Wu Wei introduces a perspective transcending dualistic tensions through syzygy, offering a holistic and integrated understanding of the individual's place within the cosmic order.

Eternal Return And Philosophical Aestheticism

Even Nietzsche's philosophies of eternal return and philosophical aestheticism hint at the possibility of truth arising from conscious-unconscious syzygy. Friedrich Nietzsche, the 19th-century German philosopher at the center of our debate, introduced the concept of eternal return, a thought experiment exploring the idea that every event in one's life would endlessly repeat in exactly the same way.

In *The Gay Science*, Nietzsche articulates this concept, stating, "What, if some day or night a demon were to steal after you into your loneliest loneliness and say to you: 'This life as you now live it and have lived it, you will have to live once more and innumerable times more; and there will be nothing new in it, but every pain and every joy and every thought and sigh and everything unutterably small or great in your life will have to return to you, all in the same succession and sequence— even this spider and this moonlight between the trees, and even this moment and I myself. The eternal hourglass of existence is turned upside down again and again, and you with it, speck of dust!'"

The notion of eternal return challenges individuals to confront the meaningfulness of their lives, urging them to live in a way that embraces the idea of eternal repetition.

Philosophical aestheticism, another key concept in Nietzsche's thought, revolves around the idea of life as a work of art. In *The Birth of Tragedy*, Nietzsche investigates the fusion of the Apollonian and Dionysian elements in art and culture, emphasizing the importance of artistic expression and the affirmation of life's inherent chaos.

He states, "We have art in order not to perish from the truth."

Nietzsche argues that art allows individuals to navigate the complexities of existence, providing a creative outlet to confront and transcend the harsh dualities of life.

Consider the tension between eternal return and the pursuit of artistic expression. In a dualistic understanding of truth, where opposing forces or principles coexist, eternal recurrence challenges individuals to confront both the light and dark aspects of their lives. The cyclic nature of eternal recurrence introduces a dynamic interplay between dualistic elements, emphasizing the repetition of both joy and suffering, pleasure and pain, and good and evil.

In this context, philosophical aestheticism functions as a compass for navigating the complexities of duality. Rather than presenting a fixed, absolute truth, Nietzsche's aestheticism suggests that truth is dynamic and multifaceted, expressed through an artistic endeavor's creative and transformative power—its teleology. Though he doesn't explicitly state it, he heavily implies it allows one to harmonize one's conscious and unconscious minds and all other paradoxical dualities that might arise from them. In a monotheistic framework, the tension between order and chaos, good and evil, can find expression through the artistic exploration of life's complexities, challenging rigid dualisms and inviting a more nuanced understanding of truth as an ever-evolving and multifaceted concept. Nietzsche's ideas, therefore, offer a unique perspective on the truth that transcends simplistic, dualistic narratives, emphasizing the creative and dynamic nature of human existence.

The Christian Logos

The concept of the Christian Logos is a central theological idea that finds its roots in the Gospel of John in the New Testament. The prologue states, "In the beginning was the Word [Logos], and the Word was with God, and the Word was God." The Logos in Christian theology represents the divine, creative, and ordering principle through which God manifests and communicates with the world. In Christian thought, the Logos is identified with Christ, the incarnate Word of God, embodying divine reason and wisdom.

Comparing the Christian Logos with the logos of ancient Greek philosophers, particularly in the context of figures like Heraclitus and the Stoics, reveals both similarities and differences. In ancient Greek philosophy, logos often referred to a cosmic principle of order and reason governing the universe. Heraclitus, for instance, saw logos as a dynamic force that harmonized opposites, stating, "This world-order [kosmos], the same of all, no god nor man did create, but it ever was and is and will be: everliving fire, kindling in measures and being quenched in measures." Similarly, the Stoics viewed logos as an immanent, rational principle guiding the cosmos.

The Christian Logos introduces a unique perspective of truth emerging from syzygy and monotheism through dualism. Within a monotheistic framework, the Christian Logos is not just a cosmic principle but a personal manifestation of the divine. Identifying the Logos with Christ introduces a relational dimension, as seen in the Gospel of John: "And the Word became flesh and dwelt among us, full of grace and truth; we have beheld his glory, glory as of the only Son from the Father." This bridges the gap between the transcendent and the immanent, providing a personal connection between God and humanity.

In terms of truth, the Christian Logos offers a synthesis of conscious-unconscious duality as syzygy by embodying the divine within the material. The tension between the eternal and the temporal, the divine and the human, is reconciled in the person of Christ as the Logos. This contrasts with some ancient Greek philosophical perspectives that may have seen the logos more as an impersonal and unconscious cosmic principle. Through its identification with Christ, the Christian Logos emphasizes a personal revelation of truth that transcends dualistic categories. The Logos becomes a unifying force, embodying truth in a way that both acknowledges and transcends the world's dualities.

Summarizing The Framework

In synthesizing the ideas expressed in this chapter, a coherent conclusion emerges that integrates natural law, the ancient Greek logos, and the Christian Logos into a discussion of truth emerging as telic synchronicity from syzygy and monotheism through dualism. The exploration of natural laws, such as the laws of thermodynamics and quantum principles, reveals an intricate dance of energy, observation, and entropy, illustrating the perpetual transformation and unpredictability of the material world. When viewed through the lens of telic synchronicity, this natural order suggests that truth is inherently dynamic, harmonizing the dualities of order and chaos, creation and destruction.

The comparison between the ancient Greek logos and the Christian Logos highlights both commonalities and distinctions. The Greek logos, as a cosmic principle of order and reason, finds resonance with the Christian Logos, which represents the divine ordering principle in Christianity. Both emphasize the underlying unity and rationality in the cosmos. However, the Christian Logos introduces a unique dimension by embodying the divine in a personal and relational form.

Drawing on the Eastern philosophy of Lao Tzu, the concept of Wu Wei adds another layer to the discussion, suggesting that harmonious alignment with the Tao, a pervasive force akin to the divine, transcends dualistic tensions. This perspective aligns with the Taoist idea that the Tao is both immanent and transcendent, providing a non-dualistic understanding of the relationship between the individual and the divine.

Nietzsche's concepts of eternal recurrence and philosophical aestheticism contribute to exploring and discovering truth beyond duality. The cyclic nature of eternal return introduces the recurrence of both joy and suffering, emphasizing the dynamic interplay of dualistic elements. Philosophical aestheticism suggests that truth is dynamic and multifaceted, expressed through artistic endeavors' creative and transformative power, challenging rigid dualisms and inviting a nuanced understanding of truth.

In conclusion, these diverse perspectives agree that truth transcends simplistic, dualistic narratives. Whether through natural laws, ancient Greek philosophy, Eastern wisdom, or Christian theology, a common thread emerges— the truth is dynamic, multifaceted, and harmonizes dualities. More concisely and precisely, truth transcends illusory duality through harmony in the conscious-unconscious mind.

The Christian Logos, in particular, offers a synthesis of duality by embodying the divine within the material, bridging the gap between the transcendent and the immanent. This understanding of truth, informed by various philosophical traditions, suggests that pursuing truth involves embracing and transcending dualities, ultimately aiming beyond dualism. According to his seminal work, *Beyond Good and Evil*, perhaps Nietzsche was right in his quest to ascend.

However, he was right for the wrong reasons. By his own admission, he strives toward immorality, declares "God is dead," entitles his work *The Antichrist*, and tries to destroy the generative principle of Christian morality, so these aren't mere accusations. No, we're taking him at his word. Therefore, why should we believe him, or anyone for that matter, who reveals such sinister motives to the world?

After all, the duality of good and evil is exactly what God warned us not to partake of with the story of Adam and Eve. Does the serpent not tempt man with blasphemous knowledge and false idols, promising transcendence yet delivering the fall? Isn't Nietzsche merely promising us the same thing as the serpent, promising a truth emerging from and transcending duality while simultaneously endeavoring to destroy the universal transcendental principle—will to truth—in pursuit of power? If so, the error in his logic should be easily revealed by following his will to power and arriving back at a universal truth beyond good and evil. That is precisely what we have shown.

Argument From Reason

Supporting this conclusion, C. S. Lewis's "Argument from Reason" provides insight into the inherent rationality of pursuing truth. Lewis argues that if naturalism is true, reason is undermined, as it would be a product of non-rational, random forces. Reasoning implies an inherent order and purpose in the universe, pointing towards a transcendent reality that grounds and supports the pursuit of truth. This argument aligns with the broader discussion, reinforcing that truth involves harmony and order transcending mere dualistic categorizations. Put another way for those who doubt Jesus was the Word incarnate or that man was made in the image of God, let them answer this question truthfully:

Does not your flesh emanate the Word of reason, and, if not reason, why should I acknowledge your irrational words, lest I, too, descend into madness? Alternatively, if your version of the word is not God but merely machinations of the flesh derived from an irrational and chaotic universe, then why should I acknowledge your godless words, lest I, too, descend into madness?

Ontological Proof

Kurt Gödel's ontological proof responds to these existential inquiries by attempting to ground the acknowledgment of God in the pure realm of logical necessity, independent of empirical or sensory experiences. By establishing the logical coherence of a maximally great being and demonstrating its necessary existence, Gödel provides a theoretical framework that transcends subjective interpretations, challenging individuals to confront the abstract nature of reason as a pathway to recognizing the existence of a transcendent deity.

Kurt Gödel (1906-1978) was an Austrian mathematician and logician renowned for his groundbreaking contributions to mathematical logic and philosophy. Born in the waning years of the Austro-Hungarian Empire, Gödel's intellectual journey unfolded during a tumultuous period marked by the aftermath of World War I and Nazi Germany's ascension. He became a central figure in the Vienna Circle, a group of philosophers and scientists exploring logical positivism. Gödel's most famous work, his incompleteness theorems, revolutionized the foundations of mathematics by demonstrating the inherent limitations within formal logical systems. Amidst this rich intellectual milieu, Gödel's ontological proof, presented in 1970, emerged as a late-career exploration into the nature of existence and divinity, reflecting his enduring fascination with logic's implications beyond the confines of mathematics. His work continues to influence diverse fields, from mathematics and philosophy to computer science, leaving an indelible mark on the 20th-century intellectual landscape.

Gödel's ontological proof of God is a complex and influential argument grounded in modal logic, aiming to establish the existence of God as a necessary consequence of logical reasoning. The proof begins by defining God as a "maximally great being" possessing all positive attributes to the highest degree. Gödel introduces a set of axioms expressing the concept of maximal greatness and utilizes modal logic to distinguish between necessary and contingent existence. The key premise asserts that if the concept of a maximally great being is logically consistent, then its existence is not merely possible but necessary. Gödel contends that the very idea of God contains inherent necessity, leading to the conclusion that God's existence is an undeniable truth within the realm of logical possibility. Here is a summarized and simplified version of Gödel's ontological proof:

Definitions:

Definition 1: *God-likeness* has essential properties that are exclusively positive.

Definition 2: *Essence* entails all and only necessary positive properties.

Definition 3: Every essence being necessarily exemplified defines *necessary existence*.

Axioms:

Axiom 1: If a property is positive, the negation is not.

Axiom 2: Any property entailed by a positive property is also positive.

Axiom 3: The property of being like God is positive.

Axiom 4: If a property is positive, it is necessarily positive.

Axiom 5: Necessary existence is positive.

Axiom 6: If a property (P) is positive, then being necessarily P is positive.

Theorems and Corollaries:

Theorem 1: Positive properties are consistent.

Corollary 1: God-likeness is consistent as a property.

Theorem 2: If something is God-like, the property of being God-like is an essence of that thing.

Theorem 3: Necessarily, the property of being God-like is exemplified.

Conclusion:

The conclusion is that God exists, derived from the theorems and definitions, particularly Theorem 3.

The Cognitive-Theoretic Model Of The Universe

On that note, let's conclude the chapter with a modern philosopher of exceptional intelligence, challenging conventional and historic wisdom with that of someone who lives day-to-day at the farthest end of the bell curve. Though his model of the universe resides along the fringe of the mainstream, we will borrow the raw computational power of his brain to tie our working philosophical framework together. Chris Langan, known for his exceptionally high IQ (speculated to be near or above 200), is a self-taught scholar who gained public attention through Malcolm Gladwell's book *Outliers*. Langan's Cognitive-Theoretic Model of the Universe (CTMU) is an encompassing theory that integrates science, philosophy, and theology. Given that the CTMU's teleology serves as a cohesive framework for these varied fields, we will utilize its metaphysical principles to refine our working framework assembled from these disciplines. The core tenets of the CTMU involve concepts such as Self-Configuring Self-Processing Language (SCSPL), syntactic operators, and a self-contained and self-defining reality. Here are several core tenets of the CTMU summarized:

1. Self-Configuring Self-Processing Language (SCSPL): The SCSPL is a fundamental concept in the CTMU. It suggests that reality is fundamentally linguistic and self-configuring. In the context of the chapter, this aligns with the exploration of truth through conscious-unconscious syzygy. The linguistic nature of reality, as proposed by SCSPL, resonates with the idea that conscious observation, internal consistency, and language play a crucial role in shaping our understanding of truth.

2. Syntactic Operators: The CTMU introduces the concept of syntactic operators, which are metaphysical linguistic entities that manipulate and process information within the framework of SCSPL. This ties into our exploration of natural laws and philosophical concepts, such as Schrödinger's Crystal and the Theory of Forms. Syntactic operators can be seen as linguistic tools that interact with the underlying fabric of reality, reflecting the interconnectedness and complexity described in the laws of thermodynamics and quantum principles.

3. Reality as Self-Configuring and Self-Defining: The CTMU posits that reality is self-configuring and self-defining through linguistic self-reference. This aligns with the chapter's exploration of truth as a dynamic and multifaceted concept emerging from conscious-unconscious syzygy. The self-configuring nature of reality, as per the CTMU, resonates with the idea that truth involves an intricate dance of conscious and unconscious elements.

4. Conscious-Unconscious Duality: The CTMU introduces the concept of duality between reality's conscious and unconscious aspects. This dualistic tension is a key theme in the CTMU. It suggests that both conscious observation and unconscious processes shape the nature of truth and reality.

5. Complexity and Interconnectedness: The CTMU emphasizes the complexity and interconnectedness of reality. This mirrors the exploration of natural laws in the chapter, particularly the intricate dance of energy, observation, and entropy. The interconnected nature of syntactic operators and their role in shaping reality aligns with the idea that truth involves a dynamic and self-sustaining process.

In Chris Langan's CTMU, syntactic operators play a crucial role in manipulating and processing information within the Self-Configuring Self-Processing Language (SCSPL) framework. Both ontologic and telic feedback mechanisms are essential components that contribute to the model's self-configuring and self-processing nature.

Ontologic feedback in the CTMU refers to the self-configuring aspect of the model, where the structure of reality adapts and configures itself based on the information and processes within the system. As linguistic entities, syntactic operators contribute to ontologic feedback by influencing how information is organized and processed in the SCSPL. This feedback mechanism reflects the dynamic and adaptive nature of the CTMU, aligning with our exploration of natural laws and philosophical concepts.

Telic feedback, conversely, pertains to the teleological or purposeful aspect of the model. It involves the consideration of goals, purposes, and intentions within the system. Syntactic operators contribute to telic feedback by serving as tools for manipulating information with specific purposes or intentions. These metaphysical linguistic entities guide information processing toward certain teleological ends, reflecting a purposeful and goal-oriented dimension within the CTMU.

Syntactic operators, as linguistic tools that interact with reality's fabric, integrate ontologic and telic feedback. They influence the self-configuration of the system while also contributing to the purposeful processing of information. This dual role aligns with the interconnectedness and complexity described by natural laws, such as those in thermodynamics and quantum principles, within the CTMU framework.

In the CTMU, individuals are conceptualized as "telors," combining the concepts of *telos* (purpose or goal) and operators. As telors, our role is to engage with the syntactic operators consciously. We play a part in the teleological feedback by using these linguistic tools with intention and purpose. The CTMU suggests that our conscious engagement with the syntactic operators influences how information is processed and the goals pursued within the system. In this sense, individuals are active participants in shaping the teleological aspects of the CTMU, contributing to its self-processing and self-configuring nature.

As telors, our fundamental role involves interacting consciously with the syntactic operators, the linguistic tools central to the CTMU's framework. Our conscious engagement with these operators is pivotal in influencing how information is processed within the system and the specific goals pursued. The CTMU posits that our conscious involvement actively shapes the teleological feedback loop, highlighting our agency in contributing to the self-processing and self-configuring nature of the theory. This perspective aligns with the CTMU's overarching principles, emphasizing the participatory and intentional role of individuals in the dynamic unfolding of the universe.

From a CTMU perspective, the human mind, with its dual conscious and unconscious aspects, is not a mere byproduct of evolutionary processes; instead, it becomes a logical imperative inherent in the self-referential and self-defining nature of the CTMU itself. The conscious-unconscious duality is not just a Darwinian adaptation but a fundamental aspect of reality's structure, where syntactic operators and teleological feedback necessitate a conscious participant for their meaningful existence.

The unconscious aspect of humanity is integrated into the framework through the concept of syntactic operators and teleological feedback. The unconscious mind, as part of the cognitive system, plays a crucial role in processing information and contributing to the overall teleology of the system. Within the CTMU, the unconscious is not relegated to a passive or secondary role; instead, it operates as an essential component engaged in the self-configuring and self-processing dynamics of the theory.

Syntactic operators function in conscious and unconscious domains. With its capacity for processing information and generating patterns beyond conscious awareness, the unconscious mind becomes a dynamic participant in shaping the teleological feedback loop. The interplay between conscious and unconscious mental processes is considered integral to the cognitive functions that contribute to the overall evolution and self-organization of the CTMU.

Psychology Of The Ctmu

In this context, the unconscious is not viewed as a mere repository of instinctual responses or evolutionary remnants. Instead, it actively participates in the ongoing self-referential and self-defining nature of the universe, contributing to the intricate dance of syntactic operators and teleological feedback that characterizes the CTMU. Integrating the unconscious into the CTMU underscores the theory's comprehensive approach to understanding reality's cognitive and teleological dimensions.

Within the CTMU, the integration of the unconscious aspect of humanity resonates with Freud's model of the psyche and Jung's concepts of the collective unconscious and archetypes. Freud's tripartite model, consisting of the id, ego, and superego, finds resonance in the CTMU's acknowledgment of syntactic operators operating at different levels of the cognitive system. Like Freud's id, the unconscious is not merely a repository of primal instincts. Still, it is intricately involved in shaping the teleological feedback loops within the CTMU.

Jung's concept of the collective unconscious, which posits the existence of shared archetypal symbols and patterns inherited by humanity, aligns with the CTMU's emphasis on syntactic operators as linguistic tools that operate collectively within the cognitive system. In both Jungian psychology and the CTMU, the unconscious transcends individual experiences, tapping into a shared reservoir of symbolic and archetypal elements that contribute to the self-organization of the cognitive system.

In the context of the CTMU, the unconscious, with its role in processing information beyond conscious awareness, becomes a nexus for the emergence of archetypal patterns and symbolic representations. These archetypes, echoing Jung's collective unconscious, participate in the ongoing self-configuring nature of the CTMU, influencing the teleological trajectory of the cognitive system.

Therefore, within the CTMU, the integration of the unconscious draws parallels with Freud's and Jung's models, providing a comprehensive framework that embraces both individual and collective dimensions of the unconscious mind in the context of syntactic operators and teleological feedback.

Ctmu In Review

In summary, the core tenets of the CTMU, such as SCSPL, syntactic operators, reality as self-configuring and self-defining, conscious-unconscious duality, and complexity and interconnectedness, encapsulate the working philosophical framework provided thus far. They contribute to the exploration of truth emerging from and transcending duality, offering a linguistic and self-referential perspective on the nature of reality. Hence, the CTMU, which emphasizes self-reference and a reality that defines itself through language, aligns with conscious-unconscious duality forming a syzygy. The SCSPL can be seen as a form of conscious expression that interacts with the underlying unconscious fabric of reality. This resonates with the conclusion that truth is discovered and actively shaped by syzygy—conscious observation and conscious-unconscious linguistic representation.

Comparing the CTMU to the natural laws discussed in the chapter, particularly the laws of thermodynamics and quantum principles, reveals a parallel in their complexity and interconnectedness. Langan's emphasis on self-reference and reality that defines itself echoes in the intricate dance of energy, observation, and entropy described in the natural laws. Both perspectives suggest a dynamic, self-sustaining, and self-resolving nature to reality.

Syzygy Conquers Schism

As our analysis of the truth concludes, a path forward involves synthesizing these ideas. Langan's CTMU, focusing on self-reference and a reality that defines itself, complements the exploration of truth through conscious-unconscious syzygy. The conscious and unconscious elements in the CTMU can be likened to the dualistic tensions explored in various philosophical traditions, such as Plato's Theory of Forms, Lao

Tzu's Wu Wei, and Nietzsche's eternal return. The integration of these diverse perspectives, along with the Christian Logos and C. S. Lewis's "Argument from Reason," suggests that truth is a dynamic, multifaceted concept transcending simplistic, dualistic narratives.

The next step involves recognizing the intricate dance of conscious and unconscious elements in shaping our understanding of truth. A more comprehensive view emerges by acknowledging the role of language, consciousness, and self-reference in defining reality. This synthesis invites a nuanced exploration of truth beyond binary categorizations, aligning with the idea that truth is a harmonious integration of dualities.

Finally, we've arrived at a comprehensive working logical and philosophical framework upon which to rest our conscious argument: truth transcends epistemology through teleology to align with ontology. Truth and goodness conquer falsehood and evil through a syzygy of ontology, epistemology, and teleology; falsehood and evil fall to truth and goodness through a schism of ontology, epistemology, and teleology. Syzygy —transcendental communication between the conscious and unconscious mind to align three heavenly bodies as one— conquers schism to reveal the truth. Thus, the will to truth starkly contrasts and transcends Nietzsche's will to power, becoming *the* truth through syzygy and resulting in telic synchronicity. For all the reasons discussed thus far, and all those we have yet to discuss, will to power is a worldview that betrays itself and all those adherent to its principles.

CHAPTER TWELVE

Syzygy and Telic Synchronicity

Aligning ontology and epistemology through teleology, we embark on a journey that traverses the vast realms of astronomy, psychology, and biblical wisdom to unravel the multifaceted tapestry of syzygy. This concept promises to illuminate the path towards transcending Nietzsche's will to power and challenging the foundations of atheism. The preceding chapter laid the groundwork for a comprehensive framework where truth and goodness triumph over falsehood and evil through the synergistic dance of ontology, epistemology, and teleology. Now, let us delve into the intricate layers of syzygy, examining it through the lenses of celestial bodies, the human psyche, and the Bible.

In the cosmos' grand symphony, the astronomical phenomenon of syzygy unfolds as a mesmerizing dance of celestial bodies coming into precise alignment. Astronomical syzygy is characterized by the straight-line configuration of three or more celestial entities, illustrating the breathtaking harmony within the cosmic order. This alignment is a metaphorical cornerstone for our argument, symbolizing the transcendental communication required to align truth, goodness, and consciousness.

A tangible example of this cosmic choreography is witnessed during solar or lunar eclipses, where the sun, Earth, and moon align so that shadows cast upon one another create a celestial spectacle. This divine alignment mirrors the synergetic revelation of truth, as the veils of falsehood and evil are temporarily eclipsed, allowing the brilliance of universal truths to shine.

As we delve deeper into the celestial realm, it becomes apparent that astronomical syzygy is not merely a physical occurrence but a profound symbol of cosmic order. The alignment of heavenly bodies reminds us of the universe's interconnectedness, where the laws governing the heavens echo the metaphysical principles underpinning our argument. The beauty of this astronomical ballet lies not only in its visual splendor but in its profound implications—a cosmic alignment that transcends the ordinary and hints at a higher, harmonious reality.

Transitioning from astronomy to psychology, syzygy takes on a psychological significance as the conscious and unconscious minds engage in a profound dialogue. In Jungian psychology, syzygy refers to the pairing of opposites within the psyche, a union that brings about transformative synthesis. The psychological syzygy is a dynamic process where opposing elements, such as the masculine and feminine archetypes, align to create a harmonious integration within the individual. This internal alignment becomes a metaphorical mirror of the cosmic dance observed in astronomical syzygy—combining disparate elements to reveal a higher truth.

The significance of psychological syzygy extends beyond individual introspection; it permeates interpersonal relationships and societal dynamics. As individuals engage in the transformative dance of aligning their inner opposites, a ripple effect occurs in the collective consciousness. Just as celestial bodies align to create cosmic harmony, psychological syzygy fosters a greater sense of unity and understanding among individuals and within society. Through the recognition and integration of opposing forces, psychological syzygy contributes to the overarching theme of our argument—truth and goodness prevailing over falsehood and evil through a syzygy resulting in telic synchronicity.

Delving deeper into Jungian psychology, the concept of synchronicity emerges as a powerful counterpart to syzygy. As defined by Jung, synchronicity refers to meaningful coincidences that conventional causality cannot explain, suggesting a deeper connection between the inner and outer worlds. Examples of synchronicity are abundant in daily life, offering glimpses into the interconnectedness of events. Consider a person contemplating a major life decision and simultaneously encountering a series of seemingly unrelated events or symbols that guide them toward a profound realization. This meaningful convergence of events transcends mere chance. It aligns with the overarching theme of our argument—the revelation of truth and goodness in telic synchronicity.

The concept of synchronicity challenges the conventional worldview by suggesting that linear cause-and-effect relationships do not solely bind events. Instead, Jungian synchronicity implies a more profound cosmic order, where the alignment of inner states and external events reveals a more profound teleology. Just as syzygy represents a cosmic alignment in the heavens, telic synchronicity signifies a meaningful alignment between individuals akin to spiritual Bluetooth, supporting our argument that truth and goodness can transcend the limitations of Nietzsche's will to power through the alignment of ontology, epistemology, and teleology.

Turning our attention to biblical perspectives, syzygy in the scriptures is manifested in the harmony of divine elements. In Genesis, the creation narrative unfolds with physical manifestations, each contributing to the cosmic order. The alignment of these divine decrees reflects a syzygy of divine will and cosmic manifestation, symbolizing the harmonious unity of truth and goodness within the framework of creation. Additionally, the biblical narrative of the Holy Trinity—Father, Son, and Holy Spirit—exemplifies a theological syzygy, where the unity of these entities encapsulates the essence of truth and goodness.

Examples of biblical syzygy are woven throughout the Bible, each illustrating divine alignments that transcend earthly divisions. The narrative of Moses receiving the Ten Commandments on Mount Sinai is a poignant example. As God aligns the moral code with divine revelation, a syzygy of moral truths is established, guiding humanity toward a higher understanding of righteousness. Moreover, the biblical concept of covenant—holy agreements between God and humanity—signifies a sacred alignment that reinforces our argument's ethical foundations. These biblical examples provide allegorical support for our overarching theme and illuminate syzygy's enduring relevance in divine revelation.

- Creation Narrative (Genesis 1): "And God said, 'Let there be light'; and there was light.'" The divine proclamation aligns with the subsequent creation of light, illustrating a syzygy of God's will and cosmic manifestation.

- The Holy Trinity (Matthew 28:19): "Go therefore and make disciples of all nations, baptizing them in the name of the Father and of the Son and of the Holy Spirit." The alignment of the three persons within the Trinity signifies a theological syzygy, embodying the unity of divine truths.

- Moses and the Ten Commandments (Exodus 20): The divine alignment of moral principles on Mount Sinai illustrates a syzygy of ethical truths, establishing a harmonious order for human conduct.

In exploring biblical syzygy, we find that the alignment of divine elements transcends the pages of scripture, echoing the cosmic theme of truth and goodness prevailing over falsehood and evil.

In conclusion, exploring astronomical, psychological, and biblical syzygy alongside Jungian synchronicity weaves a rich tapestry that supports our argument's foundational principles. Whether in the cosmic ballet of celestial bodies, the intricate dialogues within the human psyche, the divine alignments in sacred scriptures, or the meaningful coincidences of synchronicity, the essence of syzygy prevails—a profound alignment that transcends the schisms of falsehood and evil, revealing the truth in all its splendor. As we conclude our journey, these interconnected layers of syzygy and telic synchronicity will serve as the guiding light of our moral compass, illuminating the path toward a deeper understanding of the transcendent truths that unite the celestial, the psychological, and the divine.

In our argument, syzygy transcends conventional definitions, becoming a profound alignment of three nested dualities that intertwine and resonate through the fabric of existence. These dualities include: 1.) the mind and body, 2.) consciousness and unconsciousness nested in the mind, and 3.) *a priori* versus *a posteriori* arguments nested within each conscious and unconscious half. Syzygy, in this context, is the intricate dance where these dualities align in perfect harmony, creating a transcendent Gestalt that goes beyond the sum of its parts. The synchronicity inherent in syzygy is the meaningful convergence of these nested dualities in their teleology, revealing a truth surpassing each individual component's limitations.

Conversely, schism manifests as the inversion and division of the same nested dualities that syzygy harmonizes. Schism disrupts the natural alignment, creating conflicts and dissonance between mind versus body, *a priori* versus *a posteriori* interpretations of reality, and conscious versus unconscious manifestations of those interpretations. This inversion sets the stage for internal discord, leading to a fragmentation of the self and a distortion of reality. In the context of schism, the Gestalt is shattered, and synchronicity devolves into chaotic, disconnected events.

Telic synchronicity, a central concept in syzygy's triumph over schism, refers to the meaningful coincidences and interconnected events that arise from the harmonious alignment of the nested dualities. In this context, Gestalt represents the unified whole that emerges from aligning these dualities—a holistic understanding that transcends individual perspectives. Syzygy acts as a guiding force, resulting in synchronicity and a Gestalt that reveals profound truths that bridge the schisms created by the inverted and divided dualities.

At the core of our argument lies the deepest nested duality—the interplay between *a priori* and *a posteriori* arguments. The subdivisions of *a priori* include conscious rationality and unconscious faith in God. Conversely, *a posteriori* is subdivided into conscious empiricism and unconscious faith in the self. These subdivisions represent the fundamental orientations that shape our understanding of reality—whether derived from innate reasoning and faith or through empirical experience and self-reliance.

Drawing inspiration from the CTMU, *a priori* arguments, aligned with ontology, are the foundational structures of reality that exist independently of experience. *A posteriori* arguments, aligned with teleology, derive from empirical knowledge and are oriented towards the purpose or end of reality. In this framework, *a priori* becomes the fabric of existence, the "is" of reality. From the opposite perspective, *a posteriori* becomes the dynamic process, the "does" of reality.

Consider two individuals facing the complexities of existence. The first, guided by syzygy, experiences an internal consistency where the four subdivisions of *a priori* and *a posteriori* arguments harmonize. Their conscious rationality and logic align seamlessly with their unconscious faith in God, creating a union between the conscious-unconscious mind and body. This alignment leads to a state of sanity, where the Gestalt is preserved, and telic synchronicity with others guides them towards creation.

By contrast, the second individual succumbs to schism, experiencing conflicts among the four subdivisions. Their conscious and unconscious perspectives of reality are in constant turmoil, leading to a lack of internal consistency. The resulting internal discord propels them towards destruction as the Gestalt shatters, and lack of telic synchronicity devolves into chaotic happenstance and selfishness. Here, schism becomes a destructive force, unraveling the interconnectedness of the nested dualities and obscuring the path to truth.

In the culmination of our exploration into syzygy across the realms of astronomy, psychology, and biblical wisdom, we weave a novel framework anchored in the syzygy of the Holy Trinity, the synchronicity of Jungian psychology, and the telic feedback proposed by Chris Langan's Cognitive-Theoretic Model of the Universe (CTMU). This integrated framework provides a moral compass in the syzygy of the Holy Trinity but also introduces telic synchronicity—a spiritual Bluetooth connecting individuals through a common, spontaneous purpose.

The syzygy of the Holy Trinity—Father, Son, and Holy Spirit—emerges as the moral compass within our framework. This divine alignment encapsulates the essence of truth and goodness, guiding humanity. The harmonious unity within the Holy Trinity symbolizes the aligned dualities that lead to a transcendent Gestalt, offering a foundational principle for moral conduct.

Drawing inspiration from Jungian psychology and the CTMU's telic feedback, telic synchronicity is a spiritual Bluetooth—a connection between individuals guided by a common, spontaneous purpose. This synchronicity goes beyond apparent causal connections, reflecting a deeper teleological order that unites humanity. Telic synchronicity becomes the mechanism through which shared purposes manifest, fostering unity and cooperation across diverse human endeavors.

Within this framework, syzygy and teleology provide causal explanations for telic synchronicity. Just as the alignment of celestial bodies creates meaningful events in the cosmos, the alignment of human intentions, guided by the syzygy of the Holy Trinity, generates purposeful synchronicities. This newfound understanding demystifies the seemingly inexplicable occurrences of shared purpose among individuals, offering a causal link rooted in the synergetic dance of aligned dualities.

Telic synchronicity permeates every facet of human existence, from business to sports, organized religion to mass media marketing, and beyond:

- Business: A chance meeting between two entrepreneurs with complementary visions leads to creating a successful venture, showcasing telic synchronicity in the business world.
- Sports: Teammates, seemingly unrelated by background, unite with a shared goal, demonstrating telic synchronicity in sports, where the synergy of their efforts transcends individual capabilities.
- Organized Religion: The collaborative efforts of individuals within a religious community, all guided by a shared spiritual purpose, illustrate telic synchronicity in the context of organized religion.
- Mass Media Marketing and the Internet: Viral trends and phenomena across the internet, where disparate individuals contribute to a shared cultural moment, exemplify telic synchronicity in the digital age.
- Education: Collaborative breakthroughs in scientific research, where researchers from different disciplines converge on a common solution, showcase the telic synchronicity inherent in pursuing knowledge.
- Global Movements: Social and political movements that spontaneously arise, driven by shared ideals and purposes, exemplify telic synchronicity on a grand scale.

In our marvel over the wonders of modern technology, we often overlook the profound technology encoded within each individual—the syzygy embodied within us, reflecting the divine order symbolized by Adam and Eve. This framework offers a profound revelation: the potential for a unified humanity guided by shared purpose, a spiritual Bluetooth connecting us all. As we grasp the implications of this synergetic framework, we unveil a universal truth that can guide humanity into a future where the interconnected dance of our aligned dualities fosters a collective purpose. This purpose transcends the limitations of individual perspectives and leads us towards a harmonious existence.

EPILOGUE

Deconstructing the Conscious
and Unconscious Arguments

P erhaps the whole truth may encompass a somewhat contradictory duality between will to truth and will to power, best understood as a syzygy, whereby quantum states, and thus the flow of energy, are transformed differently by the conscious and unconscious. Therefore, Nietzsche's philosophies should be deconstructed using parallel conscious and unconscious methods in adherence with our journey's aim.

The Conscious Argument

In revisiting the critical points of the arguments against Nietzsche, our journey has taken us through the intricate landscapes of his philosophy, unraveling the threads of the will to power and the concept of the Übermensch. Nietzsche's unique writing style, rich with poetry, metaphors, and aphorisms, framed his arguments in a literary filigree more suited for communication with the unconscious mind. However, we encountered logical inconsistencies as we delved into the will to power. Nietzsche's attempt to shatter the foundations of Western morality and replace them with the Übermensch led to a series of contradictions and self-incriminations. For review, here are the critiques of Nietzsche's philosophy, focusing on the core tenets of the will to power and the Übermensch.

Let's highlight key arguments demonstrating the inadequacy of Nietzsche's ideas:

1. Will to Power and Self-Deception: Nietzsche contends that the will to truth expressed by previous philosophers is a facade and merely a pursuit of power for their benefit. We question whether Nietzsche's perspective on the will to power is just projection and self-incrimination. The argument suggests that Nietzsche failed to recognize a potential contradiction in his own philosophy.

2. Destruction of Morals without Clear Guidance: Nietzsche advocates for shattering the existing morals and values with a philosophical hammer, leaving the free spirits to rebuild their own set. We question the adequacy of Nietzsche's guidance, suggesting that he offered the Übermensch as a false idol without providing clear instructions for creating a new set of morals and values.

3. Logical Inconsistencies in Will to Power: Numerous logical inconsistencies in Nietzsche's concept of the will to power present themselves. We question whether Nietzsche successfully demonstrated that the will to truth is, in fact, the will to power. Our discussion touches upon the conflation of ontology and teleology, highlighting that Nietzsche may have neglected the true aim and purpose behind the will.

4. Neglect of Positive Effects of Western Morality: We argue that Nietzsche, by playing a semantic shell game, fails to acknowledge the positive effects of Western morality regardless of the creators' original intent. The critique suggests that Nietzsche's focus on the origin of values overlooks their overall intention and impact on society.

5. Failure to Understand Virtue and Ignorance: Nietzsche argues that virtues espoused by Western civilization are flawed because those who cannot adopt or

understand virtue corrupt it with ignorance. We counter this argument, suggesting that Nietzsche fails to realize that virtues may not be inherently damaged. Only their misinterpretations and misapplications are problematic.

6. Incoherence in Advocating Destruction of Morality: We question Nietzsche's logic in advocating for destroying morals and values because ignorant people can misconstrue and abuse them. The argument implies that Nietzsche's stance raises the question of why define morality at all if ignorance is an inherent aspect of human imperfection.

7. Contradiction in Übermensch Vision: We deconstruct and reconstruct Nietzsche's vision of the Übermensch multiple times, suggesting that by rebuilding it from vice, the result is an Antichrist Übermensch. When we rebuild it from a knightly-aristocratic mode of valuation, on the other hand, we ironically promote Christian virtues and the transcendental sacrifice embodied by Jesus Christ. The critique highlights the contradiction between Nietzsche's intended vision and the actual outcome, rendering his philosophy self-defeating.

8. Rejection of God's Grace: The Antichrist Übermensch, reconstructed from a literal interpretation of Nietzsche's vision, is portrayed as deliberately rejecting divine influence and moral guidance. We argue that this intentional rejection leads to a contradiction between Nietzsche's original and final vision. It symbolizes a perversion of virtues, inevitably aligning with an atheistic, nihilistic, hedonistic, and satanic ethos that dooms the literal version of the Übermensch to eternal failure.

The examination of Nietzsche's philosophy unveils a flawed perspective, where the philosopher's aim and the unintended consequences of his creations become entangled.

Nietzsche's semantic shell game, switching between "truth" and "power," leaves the reader questioning the true nature of his argument. The conscious and unconscious aspects of his philosophy appear disjointed, raising doubts about the validity of his claims.

Moreover, Nietzsche's critique of Western morality and his call for destruction reveal a failure to acknowledge its positive aspects and enduring truths. His proposed solution, the Übermensch, lacks a clear foundation and leaves followers aimless in the rubble of civilization. The attempt to construct an Übermensch from vice instead of virtue exposes the inherent contradictions in Nietzsche's vision, leading to the inadvertent creation of an Antichrist Übermensch.

This Antichrist Übermensch, characterized by a rejection of compassion, empathy, and love, starkly contrasts traditional moral principles. The deliberate choice to reject divine influence and embrace a purposeless and selfish existence represents a perversion of virtues. Nietzsche's philosophy, taken literally, seems to advocate for a world that rejects moral values, leading to a satanic ethos beyond existentialism and atheism.

As we reflect on Nietzsche and the contradictions within his philosophy, we find solace in the timeless question, "Who is like God?" The narrative turns towards a perspective aligning with the virtues associated with St. Michael: sacrifice, wisdom, and strategic thinking. The affirmation that humanity is made in the image of God, aiming towards Him, challenges Nietzsche's false proclamation of the death of God.

In response to the refutation of Nietzsche's philosophy, the conscious aim emerges as a sincere quest for a connection with God and an exploration of the divine. Instead of embracing Nietzsche's call to abandon traditional moral values and construct an aimless Übermensch, the conscious aim is to seek God as the ultimate source of truth, morality, and meaning.

The conscious pursuit of God involves a recognition of the enduring truths within Western morality that Nietzsche dismisses. It acknowledges the positive impact of virtues such as compassion, empathy, and love, which Nietzsche's proposed Antichrist Übermensch vehemently rejects. By consciously aligning with the virtues associated with Jesus Christ and drawing inspiration from biblical passages, the aim becomes clear: to seek a higher moral ground rooted in divine principles.

The conscious aim further involves a rejection of Nietzsche's satanic ethos, opting instead for a purposeful existence guided by a moral compass derived from the divine. The rejection of Nietzsche's proclamation of the death of God becomes a reaffirmation of the belief that humanity, made in the image of God, is inherently capable of aspiring toward goodness, virtue, and divine connection.

Our conscious argument articulates a response to Nietzsche's philosophy by embracing a worldview that finds meaning, purpose, and moral guidance in the divine. It involves seeking God not as a mere replacement for Nietzsche's proposed Übermensch but as the transcendent source that provides a foundation for enduring and meaningful values. Aligning the future with the divine holds profound significance, offering a transformative and purposeful orientation that contrasts with the nihilistic and relativistic implications of atheism. Here are several key aspects of aligning the future with the divine through telic synchronicity:

1. Moral Foundation and Guidance: Aligning the future with the divine establishes a moral foundation rooted in timeless and transcendent principles. Divine guidance provides a steadfast moral compass, offering a set of values that extend beyond the subjective whims of individuals or societies. This moral foundation becomes a source of stability, coherence, and shared purpose, fostering a society built on virtues such as love, compassion, and justice.

2. Meaning and Purpose: The divine offers a framework for understanding and pursuing meaning and purpose in life. By seeking alignment with divine principles, individuals can discover a sense of purpose that goes

beyond personal desires and temporal goals. This alignment provides a profound context for human existence, infusing life with significance, fulfillment, and satisfaction.

3. Community and Unity: Aligning the future with the divine encourages community and unity among individuals who share common values. It provides a basis for collective identity, fostering a shared vision for a better future. This unity extends beyond individual differences. It promotes cooperation and understanding among diverse groups as they recognize a shared connection to a higher, transcendent reality.

4. Ethical Framework for Decision-Making: Divine alignment serves as an ethical framework for decision-making at both individual and societal levels. It guides choices based on principles that are considered intrinsically good and just. This ethical foundation helps navigate the complexities of human interactions, promoting actions that contribute to the common good and the well-being of all.

5. Hope and Transcendence: Aligning the future with the divine instills a sense of hope and transcendence. The belief in a higher purpose and a divine plan offers solace during challenging times, providing a perspective that extends beyond the immediate difficulties of the present. This hope becomes a driving force for positive change, inspiring resilience and perseverance.

6. Integration of Spiritual and Material Realms: Seeking divine alignment facilitates the integration of the spiritual and material aspects of life. It encourages individuals to recognize the sacred in the ordinary, fostering a holistic understanding of existence. This integration helps overcome secular philosophies' dualism, promoting a more harmonious and

interconnected worldview.

7. Cultural and Moral Legacy: Aligning the future with the divine contributes to preserving cultural and moral legacies. By grounding values in the divine, societies can pass down a heritage that transcends temporal trends and cultural shifts. This legacy becomes a source of identity and continuity, connecting past, present, and future generations.

In summary, aligning the future with the divine through telic synchronicity offers a comprehensive framework that addresses the fundamental human need for meaning, morality, and interconnectedness. It provides a solid foundation for building a society characterized by virtues, purpose, and a shared vision of a future guided by transcendent principles.

Recognizing God represents a pivotal shift in modern philosophical, religious, and cultural perspectives, creating a nuanced framework that intertwines morality, sacrifice, and a deeper understanding of existence. Our synthesis of varied viewpoints contributes to a comprehensive argument that explores the profound implications of acknowledging the divine. This synthesis creates a robust argument that transcends disciplinary boundaries. Philosophical rigor meets religious devotion, and cultural norms find a deeper justification. By recognizing the divine, syzygy bridges the perceived gaps between reason and faith, providing a holistic framework for understanding the complexities of human existence. God is not merely an abstract concept but a living reality that informs and shapes human conduct.

Embracing a future aligned with the divine constitutes the conscious aim of this exploration. In recognizing God as the guiding force, the conscious aim is to forge a path toward a higher understanding of existence and morality. This alignment with the divine is not merely a spiritual or religious pursuit; it involves a conscious decision to integrate the divine into the fabric of individual and collective aspirations using a natural, spiritual Bluetooth. By consciously aligning with

God, individuals seek to navigate life's complexities with a collective moral compass grounded in transcendent principles. This conscious aim sets the stage for a transformative journey toward God, encompassing philosophical, religious, and cultural dimensions.

Introducing the Cognitive-Theoretic Model of the Universe (CTMU) as a framework for understanding the divine adds depth and coherence to the conscious aim. The CTMU provides a unique perspective that transcends traditional disciplinary boundaries, offering a comprehensive model that addresses the ontology, epistemology, and teleology of reality. This framework goes beyond conventional philosophical and theological paradigms, introducing a language of reality that incorporates the structure of existence (ontology), our human limitations in understanding that structure (epistemology), and the purposeful evolution of reality (teleology). By incorporating the CTMU into the conscious aim, individuals gain a sophisticated tool to navigate the complexities of aligning with the divine, fostering a deeper understanding of the interplay between consciousness, existence, and the ultimate aim of existence—God.

The CTMU introduces profound principles that underpin its unique perspective on reality. At its core, the CTMU incorporates ontologic and telic feedback, providing a framework that seamlessly integrates the structure and purpose of the universe. Ontologic feedback refers to the self-defining nature of reality, where the form of existence is inseparable from the definition process. On the other hand, telic feedback addresses the purposeful evolution of reality, emphasizing that the end goals of existence are inherently connected to the ongoing process of becoming. This dual feedback system offers a nuanced understanding of how the universe operates, highlighting the inseparability of its structure and purpose.

Syntactic operators play a crucial role in the CTMU by providing a formal language for describing the relationships and transformations within the universe. These operators allow for the precise articulation of complex concepts, enabling a more accurate representation of reality. Additionally, telors, defined as goals or purposes inherent in the structure of reality, introduce a teleological dimension to the model. Telors act as attractors, guiding the universe's evolution toward specific end-states by acting as purposeful entities that influence events unfolding in the temporal domain—past, present, and future. In terms of time, telors operate across the temporal spectrum. They are not confined to a linear timeline but holistically engage with the past, present, and future. Telors contribute to the shaping of events in the past by influencing the information structure that defines historical reality. In the present, they actively participate in the ongoing process of reality construction. Importantly, telors guide the universe's evolution toward specific end-states or telic goals by interacting with the future through timeless syntactic operators.

Understanding the significance of syntactic operators and the role of telors is crucial in grasping the intricacies of the CTMU, as they form the language through which the model articulates the dynamic interplay between structure and purpose within the cosmic framework. More significantly, it answers profound questions: why are we here, and what is our purpose? As part of a self-defining, self-referencing universe akin to God, we are here to define and transform that universe through telic feedback—our aim. Thus, without us, existence could not exist as it exists.

The Unconscious Argument

The allegory serves as the unconscious underpinning of our exploration, providing a symbolic narrative that parallels and enriches the conscious argument. In the arduous journey of the man burdened by the dragon's demand for an annual tithe, we find a canvas upon which deeper philosophical and psychological themes are painted. This allegory unfolds as a dreamlike narrative, with each element representing facets of the human psyche and the quest for a transcendent understanding. As we delve into the symbolic representations within this allegory, we uncover layers of meaning that bridge the realms of consciousness and the unconscious to form a syzygy.

The allegory's symbolic representations are intricate and layered, reflecting psychological archetypes and the dynamics of the collective unconscious. The camel, burdened by the weight of gold and transformed from a man, symbolizes the individual's struggle to carry the collective burdens imposed by external forces like the dragon, mirroring Freud's superego concept. With its cunning temptation and offer of an alternative path, the fox embodies the trickster archetype, akin to Jung's notion of the shadow aspect. At the same time, his mask represents the persona we reveal to the outside world. The lion, realizing its true nature beneath the deceptive masks of the persona, aligns with the individuation process, a central concept in Jungian psychology.

The serpent, acting as a revealer of truth and orchestrator of the man's transformation, resonates with the archetype of change and knowledge, reminiscent of Jung's depiction of the anima or animus and their syzygy. In a biblical context, the anima and animus are akin to Adam and Eve, and the serpent's temptation in the Garden of Eden adds another layer of complexity by bringing them into consciousness. The dragon, a false god demanding worship and sacrifice, mirrors Freud's superego, Nietzsche's critique of conventional morality, and the idea of the Übermensch transcending good and evil. The hanging man, a sacrificial figure, echoes religious and mythological themes, such as Odin's sacrifice for runes or Jesus's sacrifice on the cross, representing the suffering required for redemption. Lastly, the phoenix emerging from sacrifice signifies renewal and transformation, illustrating the cyclical nature of life and death inherent in Jung's concept of the transcendent function arising from the syzygy.

Once revered as a god demanding sacrifice, the dragon is

unveiled as a deceptive force, akin to Nietzsche's proclamation that "God is dead." The dragon's demand for a tithe symbolizes blind adherence to oppressive systems, echoing the unconscious struggle against false gods and societal expectations. The revelation of the serpent, exposing the dragon's deceit and offering an alternative path, aligns with the Nietzschean idea of transcending imposed values. The allegory reflects the unconscious striving for authenticity and the overthrowing of false authorities.

Moreover, the dragon's attempt to maintain control through deception draws parallels with Nietzsche's Übermensch, who breaks free from societal illusions. The serpent's role in stealing the apple and exposing the dragon's manipulation is a metaphor for the unconscious forces that disrupt conventional narratives. The allegory thus invites us to reconsider the nature of authority and divinity, prompting a conscious shift toward a more authentic and self-determined existence in alignment with God.

Toward the end of the allegory, the mirror is a powerful tool for revelation and self-discovery. Reflecting the lion positioned between the dragon and the serpent, it becomes a symbolic portal through which the protagonist gains insight into the dragon's power and the nature of existence. Reflecting past, present, and future, the mirror aligns with Freud's concept of the unconscious, revealing hidden aspects of the self. It also resonates with Jung's idea of the syzygy, representing the bridge between the conscious and unconscious realms. The protagonist's confrontation with his reflection, hanging from the tree, underscores the existential struggle and the unveiling of uncomfortable truths. The mirror becomes a metaphor for the introspective journey, forcing the protagonist to confront his own illusions and false perceptions.

The descent into the abyss symbolizes the protagonist's journey into the depths of the unconscious, mirroring Jung's concept of individuation. As the lion follows the serpent into the abyss, it reflects the psychological descent into the darker aspects of the self. The revelation of the dragon's power, coiled around the apple tree, illustrates the hidden forces that shape human behavior and consciousness. The abyss becomes a metaphor for the unknown, representing the fears and uncertainties inherent during self-discovery. The encounter with the dragon's magical mirror, revealing the interconnectedness of all aspects of existence, reinforces the idea that true understanding requires confronting both light and shadow. The descent and subsequent revelation mark a pivotal point in the protagonist's transformation, highlighting the necessity of grappling with the unconscious to achieve a more authentic and enlightened state of being.

The allegory seamlessly aligns with CTMU principles, offering a lens through which the protagonist's conscious and unconscious choices can be analyzed. The journey from camel to lion and the subsequent descent into the abyss mirror the ontologic feedback loop, where the protagonist undergoes a process of self-transformation and self-realization. The conscious aim, explicitly stated as embracing a future aligned with the divine, resonates with the telic feedback inherent in the CTMU. The protagonist's choices reflect the syntactic operators at play, manipulating the narrative of his existence. The fox, serpent, and dragon become symbolic representations of the telors, introducing choices and alternate paths that contribute to unfolding the protagonist's journey and purpose. The allegory, therefore, serves as a microcosm of the CTMU principles, illustrating how self-reference, aim, and syntactic operations interweave in the fabric of the protagonist's journey toward a divine future.

From the perspective of the CTMU, the utilization of an unconscious argument finds justification within the framework of syntactic operators and transcending conscious-unconscious duality through syzygy. The CTMU posits that reality, as a self-processing entity, is fundamentally syntactic, governed by a language-like structure that involves the manipulation of symbols and information. Within this syntactic framework, consciousness is considered a specialized form of self-reference. The unconscious, by contrast, represents the vast reservoir of information and potential within the system. Syntactic operators, the dynamic mechanisms of information manipulation, extend beyond the dichotomy of conscious and unconscious, operating at the core of reality itself. By employing an unconscious argument, one taps into the syntactic depth of the system, acknowledging that the conscious mind is but a subset of a larger, self-referential structure. In this way, the CTMU justifies integrating unconscious elements into the argument, recognizing them as integral to the holistic understanding of reality's self-processing nature.

Jung's theory of the collective unconscious and Plato's Theory of Forms resonate with the CTMU in the context of reality as a self-contained, self-referential system. Jung's collective unconscious posits a shared reservoir of universal symbols and archetypes that are part of the human experience, accessible to individuals through dreams, myths, and cultural symbols. According to Jung, this collective layer of the mind connects individuals to a broader, shared human experience.

Jungian archetypes, representing universal, symbolic patterns in the collective unconscious, find resonance in the allegory's symbolic characters—the camel, fox, mask, lion, serpent, dragon, magic mirror, hanging man, and phoenix. These archetypes, like Jung's collective unconscious, contribute to the deeper layers of meaning and transformation within the allegory, reflecting universal aspects of the human psyche and its journey toward individuation.

Similarly, Plato's philosophy, particularly his Theory of Forms, suggests that abstract, non-material ideals or archetypes exist beyond the physical world and are accessible through intellectual contemplation. Plato's realm of Forms implies a transcendent reality of perfect, timeless entities that shape the imperfect manifestations in the material world. This aligns with the CTMU's notion of ontologic feedback and the self-contained nature of reality. The allegory's symbolic representations are imperfect reflections of higher, archetypal forms, resonating with Plato's idea of the eternal and unchanging realm of Forms.

The CTMU, with its emphasis on a self-contained reality grounded in syntactic structure, aligns with these perspectives by acknowledging the existence of a foundational, self-referential syntax that underlies both individual and collective consciousness. The CTMU's syntactic operators, serving as the dynamic components of reality's self-processing, resonate with Jung's archetypes and Plato's Forms in their capacity to shape and influence the expressions within the system. In the context of the CTMU, Jungian archetypes, Plato's Theory of Forms, biblical representations of the Holy Trinity, and Freud's model of the psyche can be integrated into the larger argument, providing a psychological dimension to the interplay between the conscious and unconscious aspects of reality.

Freud's model of the psyche, consisting of the conscious, unconscious, and preconscious mind, aligns with the CTMU's emphasis on the relationship between conscious and unconscious aspects of reality. In our argument, the deliberate aim toward God is analogous to Freud's conscious mind, representing our journey's intentional and self-aware aspect. Meanwhile, the unconscious argument, depicted through the allegory and symbolic representations, corresponds to Freud's unconscious mind, representing hidden motivations, desires, and the transformative journey.

Freud's model of the psyche can be metaphorically related to the Holy Trinity by drawing parallels between its three components—the conscious, unconscious, and preconscious mind—and the three persons of the Holy Trinity—Father, Son, and Holy Spirit.

1. The Conscious Mind and the Father:
   a. Freud's Conscious Mind: This represents surface-level awareness, intentional thought processes, and rational decision-making. It is akin to the conscious mind in our argument,

which is actively pursuing the divine—the conscious aim toward God.

  b. Parallel with the Father: In the Holy Trinity, the Father is often associated with God's intentional and authoritative aspect. Similarly, the conscious mind, through its intentional pursuits and decisions, reflects the role of the Father in Freud's model.

2. The Unconscious Mind and the Son:

  a. Freud's Unconscious Mind: This represents the hidden, deeper layers of the psyche, housing repressed memories, desires, and transformative elements. It corresponds to the unconscious argument in our narrative, symbolized by the allegory and its transformative journey.

  b. Parallel with the Son: In the Holy Trinity, the Son is often associated with God's redemptive and transformative aspect, symbolizing the divine entering into the human experience. Similarly, the unconscious mind reflects transformative processes and hidden elements, aligning with the redemptive narrative in the allegory.

3. The Preconscious Mind and the Holy Spirit:

  a. Freud's Preconscious Mind: This lies between the conscious and unconscious, holding information that is not immediately accessible but can be brought into consciousness. It can be compared to the transitional elements in our argument, where the protagonist's journey involves transitions between conscious and unconscious states.

  b. Parallel with the Holy Spirit: The Holy Spirit, often associated with guidance and influence, can be paralleled with the preconscious mind's role in providing information and influencing conscious awareness, as well as syntactic operators in the CTMU. Both play intermediary roles in facilitating understanding and connection.

While Freud's model was not explicitly designed to mirror religious concepts like the Holy Trinity, these parallels offer an imaginative and metaphorical connection between psychological frameworks and theological concepts. This alignment underscores the richness of the interplay between psychological and spiritual dimensions within our overarching argument.

The Holy Trinity, a central concept in Christianity, posits the Father, Son, and Holy Spirit as three distinct persons in one Godhead. In our argument, the conscious aim toward God can be associated with the Father, representing the intentional pursuit of divine alignment. The symbolic journey and transformations depicted in the allegory parallel the redemptive narrative often associated with the Son. At the same time, the transformative and guiding role of the CTMU's telors and syntactic operators aligns with the Holy Spirit's influence on the unfolding of divine purposes.

In the CTMU, *triality* is a fundamental concept that integrates three logically interdependent aspects or categories, forming a self-referential and self-contained system. This triadic structure can be compared to the Holy Trinity in Christian theology, where the Father, Son, and Holy Spirit exist in a unified yet distinct relationship. In the CTMU, triality is not a direct replica of the Holy Trinity but shares conceptual similarities. Triality in the CTMU comprises the categories of syntax, extension, and intension, forming a self-generating, self-processing reality reminiscent of the interdependence within the Holy Trinity.

Regarding the role of God in the CTMU, God is defined as the ultimate self-aware and self-designating entity within the system. God represents the totality of reality and consciousness, encompassing all categories of existence. God is not an external entity but rather the self-contained, self-defining essence that constitutes the very fabric of the universe. This perspective aligns with a pantheistic understanding, where God is immanent in the structure and dynamics of reality itself. The CTMU's concept of God goes beyond traditional anthropomorphic depictions. It emphasizes a unified, self-contained, and self-aware foundation of existence.

In the context of the CTMU, the ancient Greek concept of "logos" and the Christian understanding of the "Logos" find resonance in the framework of triality and self-reference. The Greek term "logos" encapsulates notions of order, reason, and discourse, representing a principle of cosmic order and intelligence. In the CTMU, logos aligns with the syntactic component of triality, representing the rule-based, self-referential structure that defines reality.

Similarly, in Christian theology, the Logos describes the divine principle of order and knowledge, often identified with Christ. Within the CTMU, the Christian Logos can be conceptually linked to the triality's syntactic component, representing the intelligent, self-aware aspect of the ultimate reality. In Greek and Christian traditions, Logos implies a fundamental ordering principle that shapes the universe's structure.

Moreover, the CTMU's emphasis on self-reference and self-awareness in its triadic structure aligns with the Christian understanding of the Logos as a divine intelligence that not only orders the cosmos but also embodies a self-aware and self-referential aspect of the divine. In this way, the ancient Greek logos and Christian Logos find a conceptual bridge within the CTMU's framework, emphasizing the role of an intelligent, self-referential order in the fabric of reality.

In the broader argument, Freud's model of the psyche serves as a psychological framework, Jungian archetypes contribute symbolic depth, Plato's Theory of Forms adds metaphysical context, and the Holy Trinity provides a religious and spiritual dimension. These elements collectively enrich the exploration of the conscious and unconscious realms, the symbolic journey toward God, and the teleological aspects guided by the principles of the CTMU. The integration of these perspectives creates a comprehensive understanding of the interconnectedness of psychological, metaphysical, and spiritual dimensions within the context of our argument.

Coming to our conclusion, the protagonist's awakening in paradise culminates in a transformative journey, symbolizing transcendence and spiritual enlightenment. As he blinks in disbelief at the flourishing gardens around him, the once barren desert replaced by abundance, the man experiences a profound realization. This moment represents a physical change in the landscape and, more importantly, a metaphysical evolution within himself. The paradise mirrors the internal paradise he has discovered through the trials of the allegorical quest. The spiritual awakening underscores the idea that the journey, with all its sacrifices and revelations, has led to a higher understanding and connection with divine principles.

The symbolism of the golden gateway opening marks a pivotal moment in the protagonist's spiritual journey. The gate, adorned in gold, represents a threshold to a higher plane of existence and spiritual enlightenment. Its opening signifies the protagonist's readiness to enter a new phase of understanding and reality. The gold, once associated with the dragon's oppressive lordship, now becomes a symbol of transcended power and divine knowledge. The act of the gateway opening reflects the protagonist's internal growth and readiness to share the newfound wisdom—embodied in the dragon's scales inscribed with God's law—with his people. This moment encapsulates the idea that enlightenment is not solely an individual achievement but a gift to be shared for the betterment of the collective.

The protagonist's symbolic act of bringing the dragon's scales, inscribed with God's law, back to his people is laden with transformative power and significance. The dragon's scales, once a symbol of oppression and false godhood, now carry the weight of divine wisdom. By delivering these scales to his community, the protagonist becomes a bearer of transcendent knowledge, offering his people a chance at liberation from the oppressive dragon-like forces in their lives. This act underscores the theme of sacrifice and redemption, as the protagonist utilizes the lessons learned on his journey to guide and elevate others. The closing of the golden gates behind him signifies both the completion of his personal quest and the preservation of the newfound paradise—a testament to the enduring impact of the transformative journey on the individual and the community.

In the poignant dialogue with God, the protagonist seeks forgiveness and understanding for his actions throughout the allegorical journey. Existential inquiries come to the forefront as he questions God about the inevitability of his choices, grappling with the concept of free will and divine knowledge. The dialogue delves into the complexities of human agency within a framework of predestined outcomes, echoing the broader philosophical implications explored in the conscious argument. It becomes a moment of profound introspection as the protagonist grapples with the consequences of his choices and seeks reconciliation with the divine force that orchestrated his journey. This dialogue bridges the conscious and unconscious realms as the protagonist confronts the essence of his existence.

The release of the fiery arrow is the protagonist's final act of repentance and surrender. Not only does it symbolize a relinquishing of the dragon's power acquired throughout the allegory, but it also represents a purifying sacrifice. The flaming arrow, launched toward heaven, embodies the protagonist's acknowledgment of the consequences of his actions and a desire for redemption. The fire, a recurring motif throughout the allegory, plays a dual role here, signifying destruction and renewal. This act of repentance transcends the individual, carrying collective implications as the protagonist relinquishes power in the name of a higher purpose. The symbolism of the flaming arrow and its transformation into a phoenix resonates with themes of resurrection and spiritual rebirth.

The protagonist's transformation into a phoenix serves as the climax of his journey, representing a profound metamorphosis and rebirth. As the phoenix disappears beyond the horizon, it symbolizes the transcendence of earthly limitations and the attainment of spiritual liberation. The phoenix, a mythical creature associated with immortality and renewal, embodies the transformative potential of sacrifice and repentance. The horizon, often a symbol of the unknown and the future, becomes a metaphorical threshold, suggesting that the protagonist's spiritual journey extends beyond the immediate narrative. The phoenix's flight into the sun's glare implies a merging with celestial forces, transcending the earthly realm. This transformation encapsulates the overarching theme of the conscious argument—redefining the aim toward God through syzygy—and provides a visually evocative conclusion to the allegorical narrative.

The man, now transformed and enlightened by the arduous journey, walks into paradise carrying the dragon's scales—a symbolic representation of God's law. The paradisiacal setting, born from the ashes of the allegorical struggle, becomes the culmination of the protagonist's quest for divine understanding. As he steps through the golden gates, the act becomes a profound symbol of completion and attainment. Once a burden and a representation of false authority, the dragon's scales now serve as a vessel for newfound wisdom to be shared with the people. Closing the golden gates behind the man marks the end of the transformative journey, creating a sense of closure and separation between the earthly and the divine.

Our transformative journey, woven through the conscious and unconscious arguments, concludes by reflecting on its profound themes and lessons. At its core, the narrative explores the complexities of human agency, the interplay between conscious and unconscious forces, and the pursuit of the divine within and beyond oneself. The protagonist's trials, represented by the allegory's symbolic characters and events, serve as a microcosm of the broader human experience. Themes of sacrifice, repentance, and transcendence emerge as central motifs, emphasizing the cyclical nature of spiritual growth. The overarching moral gleaned from the allegory is recognizing that the pursuit of God is not a linear path but a continuous, multifaceted journey that requires introspection, sacrifice, and a willingness to confront both conscious and unconscious aspects of the self. This epilogue invites you to contemplate the significance of the protagonist's newfound wisdom and its potential impact on the collective understanding of God.

Now ask yourself again: Who is like God? What will you do when your time comes, and you must sacrifice for Him?

REFERENCES

1. Thomas Nelson. (1971). *The Holy Bible: Revised Standard Version Containing the Old and New Testaments* (2nd ed.; reference).
2. Nietzsche, F. W., & Hollingdale, R. J. (1969). *Thus Spoke Zarathustra: A Book for Everyone and No One* (Repr. with new chronology and further reading 2003). Penguin.
3. Dante, A., & Cary, H. F. (1880). *The Vision: Or Hell Purgatory and Paradise of Dante Alighieri*. American Book Exchange.
4. Crawford, J. (2019). *The Wanderer's Hávamál*. Hackett Publishing Company.
5. 宮本 武蔵 & Wilson, W. S. (2002). *The Book of Five Rings* (1st ed.). Kodansha International.
6. Sunzi, S., Giles, L., & Phillips, T. R. (2019). *The Art of War*. IXIA Press.
7. Confucius, C., & Chin, A.-ping. (2014). *The Analects = Lunyu*. Penguin Books.
8. Machiavelli, Niccolò, Ricci, L. Vincent, Detmold, C. E., & Lerner, M. (1940). *The Prince and The Discourses*. Modern Library.
9. Marcus, A., Hammond, M., & Clay, D. (2006). *Meditations*. Penguin Books.
10. Atkins, P. W. (2010). *The Laws of Thermodynamics: A Very Short Introduction*. Oxford University Press. Retrieved December 24, 2023, from http://site.ebrary.com/id/10464130.
11. Sen, D. (2014). "The uncertainty relations in quantum mechanics." Current Science, 107(2), 203–218.
12. Dirac, P.A.M. (1967). *The Principles of Quantum*

Mechanics (4th ed.). Oxford University Press, p. 3.

13. Shankar, R. (1994). *Principles of Quantum Mechanics.* Plenum Press, New York. http://dx.doi.org/10.1007/978-1-4757-0576-8.

14. Descartes, R. (2008). *Meditations on First Philosophy* (M. Moriarty, Trans.). Oxford University Press.

15. Plato, P., & Jowett, B. (2020). *Plato: Complete Works.*

16. Plato. (1925). *Plato in Twelve Volumes,* Vol. 9 translated by Harold N. Fowler. Cambridge, MA, Harvard University Press; London, William Heinemann Ltd.

17. Laozi, L., Ong, Y.-P., Müller, Charles, & Stade, G. (2005). *Tao Te Ching.* Barnes & Noble Classics.

18. Nietzsche, F. W., & Kaufmann, W. A. (1974). *The Gay Science: With a Prelude in Rhymes and Appendix of Songs.* Vintage Books.

19. Krell, D. F. (1976). "Art and Truth in Raging Discord: Heidegger and Nietzsche on the Will to Power." Boundary 2, 379–392. https://doi.org/10.2307/302141.

20. Warren, J., & Sheffield, F. C. C. (2014). *The Routledge Companion to Ancient Philosophy.* Routledge/Taylor & Francis Group.

21. Nietzsche, F. W., & Kaufmann, W. (1989). *Beyond Good and Evil: Prelude to a Philosophy of the Future.* Vintage Books.

22. Nietzsche, F. W., Ridley, A., & Norman, J. (2010). *The Anti-Christ; Ecce Homo; Twilight of the Idols: And Other Writings* (6th ed.). Cambridge University Press.

23. Lewis, C. S. (2001). *Miracles: A Preliminary Study* (1st HarperCollins pbk.). HarperOne.

24. Gödel, K. (1995). *Ontological Proof.* In S. Feferman & J. W. Dawson Jr. (Eds.), *Collected Works: Volume III, Unpublished Essays and Lectures.* Oxford University Press.

25. Langan, C. M. (2002). *Introduction to the CTMU.* In

E. R. Eddington (Ed.), *Cognitive-Theoretic Model of the Universe: A New Kind of Reality Theory* (pp. 1–18).

26. Freud, S. (1923). *The Ego and the Id*. In J. Strachey (Ed. and Trans.), *The Standard Edition of the Complete Psychological Works of Sigmund Freud* (Vol. 19, pp. 3–66).

27. Jung, C. G. (1959). *The Archetypes and the Collective Unconscious* (R. F. C. Hull, Trans.). In H. Read et al. (Eds.), *The Collected Works of C. G. Jung* (Vol. 9i). Routledge.

28. Jung, C. G. (1959). *Aion: Researches into the Phenomenology of the Self* (R. F. C. Hull, Trans.). In H. Read et al. (Eds.), *The Collected Works of C. G. Jung* (Vol. 9ii). Routledge.

29. Jung, C. G. (1958). *The Structure and Dynamics of the Psyche* (R. F. C. Hull, Trans.). In H. Read et al. (Eds.), *The Collected Works of C. G. Jung* (Vol. 8). Routledge.

30. Jung, C. G. (1960). *Synchronicity: An Acausal Connecting Principle* (R. F. C. Hull, Trans.). In H. Read et al. (Eds.), *The Collected Works of C. G. Jung* (Vol. 8). Routledge.

Made in the USA
Las Vegas, NV
22 January 2024

84754657R00114